BY PRACTICE, BY INVI
Design Practice Resear
Architecture and Desigr
1986–2011

COLOPHON

By Practice, By Invitation
Design Practice Research in Architecture
and Design at RMIT, 1986-2011
The Pink Book (Third Edition)

Published by
Actar Publishers, New York, Barcelona
www.actar.com

Edited by
Leon van Schaik, Anna Johnson
Revisions to Third Edition — Ian
Nazareth

Design and Typeset
Stuart Geddes and Alex Margetic
with thanks to Wei Huang

With contributions by
Kate Heron, Li Shiqiao, Allan Powell,
Howard Raggatt, Carey Lyon, Ian
McDougall, John Wardle, Jennifer Lowe,
SueAnne Ware, Richard Blythe, Martyn
Hook, Michael Trudgeon, Sand Helsel,
Vivian Mitsogianni, m3architecture,
Nigel Bertram, Paul Minifie, Charles
Anderson, Richard Black, Stephen
Collier, Graham Crist, Thomas Daniell,
Melanie Dodd, Theodore Krueger III,
Rosalea Monacella, Nicholas Murray,
Yael Reisner

Copy editing and proofreading
Ellen Jensen

Printing and binding
Tiger Printing (Hong Kong)

Distribution
Actar D, Inc. New York, Barcelona.

New York
440 Park Avenue South, 17th Floor
New York, NY 10016, USA
T +1 2129662207
salesnewyork@actar-d.com

Barcelona
Roca i Batlle 2-4
08023 Barcelona, Spain
T +34 933 282 183
eurosales@actar-d.com

Indexing
English ISBN: 978-1-948765-17-6
PCN: Library of Congress Control
Number: 2019932194

Printed in China

Publication date: April 2019

BY PRACTICE, BY INVITATION:
Design Practice Research in Architecture and Design at RMIT, 1986–2011

(THE PINK BOOK)

Allan Powell
Howard Raggatt
Carey Lyon
Ian McDougall
John Wardle
Jennifer Lowe
SueAnne Ware
Richard Blythe
Martyn Hook
Michael Trudgeon
Sand Helsel
Vivian Mitsogianni
m3architecture

Nigel Bertram
Paul Minifie

Charles Anderson
Richard Black
Stephen Collier
Graham Crist
Thomas Daniell
Melanie Dodd
Theodore Krueger III
Rosalea Monacella
Nicholas Murray
Yael Reisner

THIRD EDITION

Leon van Schaik and
Anna Johnson

Essay by
Leon van Schaik

Forewords by
Kate Heron and
Li Shiqiao

Design Practice Research at RMIT University is a longstanding program of research into what venturous designers actually do when they design. It is probably the most enduring and sustained body of research of its kind: empirical, evidence-based and surfacing evidence about design practice. It is a growing force in the world, with a burgeoning program of research in Asia, Oceania and Europe. This book documents some of its past achievements.

Two kinds of knowledge are created by the research. One concerns the ways in which designers marshal their intelligence, especially their spatial intelligence, to construct the mental space within which they practice design. The other reveals how public behaviours are invented and used to support design practice. This new knowledge combined is the contribution that this research makes to the field of design practice research.

Perhaps the most notable feature of this research program is the gathering together of all candidates in biannual Research Symposia. Originally these were named Graduate Research Conferences (GRCs). They are now named Practice Research Symposia (PRS). In this edition we refer to them as Research Symposia.

This twenty-five-year long program of research has relied on the incremental creation of a team of colleagues. In the early years, Peter Downton and Sand Helsel were crucial members of the team, as they still are. Later, as the research shifted into PhD mode, they were joined by external advisers Ranulph Glanville, Paul Carter and Nikos Papastergiadis. Since the mid-2000s, the team of supervisors has grown to include SueAnne Ware, Martyn Hook, Richard Blythe, Sand Helsel and Vivian Mitsogianni, and soon to join these are Richard Black, Graham Crist, Melanie Dodd and Paul Minifie.

Craig Bremner, Lindsay Anderson, Shane Murray, Nigel Bertram, Gini Lee and Thomas Daniell (the latter two of whom won the Vice Chancellor's Award for the best PhD in their year) all now hold significant academic positions in other universities.

Not covered by this volume, therefore, are those recently completed or currently enrolled:

Anton James	Harold Fallon
Arnaud Hendrickx	James McAdam
Belinda Winkler	Jan van Schaik
C.J. Lim	Johan Van Den Berghe
Cameron Bruhn	Jon Tarry
Chris Morgan	Kate Cullity
Corneel Cannaerts	Katica Pedisic
Deborah Saunt	Kevin Taylor (posthumous)
Denise Sprynskyi	Lucas Devriendt
Dianne Peacock	Matthew Bird
Ephraim Joris	Perry Lethlean
Gretchen Wilkins	Peter Boyd

Peter Macfarlane
Petra Pferdmenges
Riet Eeckhout
Sébastien Penfornis
Tan Kok Hiang

Tanya Kalinina
Thierry Kandjee
Tom Holbrook
Veronica Valk

The program has been externally reviewed by visiting critics, whose role has been vital to the quality of the investigations. We are enormously grateful to them for their time, and for their feedback, some of which is recorded in the Plenary Comments. Two of these have contributed forewords detailing why they see the research as significant: Li Shiqiao and Kate Heron. One has contributed a postscript pointing to the way ahead: Johan Verbeke. All our visiting critics seem to be energised by and to enjoy their engagement with the program.

Anna Johnson carried out the research for and wrote the case studies in the book, and we are grateful to those interviewed for their time. We plan future volumes of excerpts from the research catalogues of all completed Invitational Program PhDs. These volumes will join the published research catalogues of those who worked through the program at research Master's level (see Bibliography).

This edition copy-edited by Ellen Jensen.

Initial archival research by Peta Carlin.

Research Assistant: Melisa McDonald.

In consultation with Leon van Schaik, the process for revising this third edition was managed by Ian Nazareth, School of Architecture and Design.

Leon van Schaik AO
RMIT, October 2018

Since the second edition two major grants have been initiated and acquitted by RMIT, the originator of this mode of research; and these have disseminated our model of practice reflection research by practitioners with a recognised body of work meriting such reflection.

A Marie Curie grant in the European Union's Seventh Framework Programme for research, technological development and demonstration (no. 317 325). Known as ADAPTr this involved these institutions:

→ RMIT School of Architecture and Design (now Architecture and Urban Design)
→ KU Leuven
→ Aarhus School of Architecture
→ Estonian Academy of Arts
→ The Glasgow School of Art
→ University of Ljubljana
→ University of Westminster

And an Australian OLT (Office for Learning and Teaching) grant entitled Design and Architecture Practice Research and known as DAPr. This was a RMIT led collaboration between 14 Australian Universities – involving academics from all the schools of architecture in the country.

In addition, Professor Michael McGarry has instituted a thriving and exemplary stream at Queens University Belfast.

The following practitioners have completed PhDs in the program, and their work can be seen on the research repository at RMIT:

→ https://practice-research.com/

and their examinations can be viewed on vimeo at

→ https://vimeo.com/user3911530

Anderson, B (AUS)	Van Schaik, Jan (AUS)
Byrne, Denis (IR)	Tarry, John (AUS)
Baracco, Mauro (AUS)	Hoete, Anthony (NZ)
Attiwill, Suzie (AUS)	Sprynskji, Denise (AUS)
Casey, Alice (IR)	Crist, Graham (AUS)
Bette, Urs (AUS)	Holbrook, Tom (UK)
Bertram, Nigel (AUS)	Guitierrez, Laurent (V)
Clancy, Andrew (IR)	Fallon, Harold (B)
Bird, Matthew (AUS)	Kanjee, Thiery (B)
Black, Richard (AUS)	James, Anton (AUS)
Cody, Peter (IR)	Hendrickx, Arnaud (B)
Boyd, Peter (AUS)	Larkin, Steve (IR)
Collier, Stephen (AUS)	Johnson, Anna (AUS)
DeVriendt, Lucas (B)	Minifie, Paul (AUS)
Dodd, Mel (UK)	Lim, CJ (UK)
Van Den Berghe, Johan (B)	Kovac, Tom (AUS)
Eeckhout, Riet (B)	Mitsogianni, Vivian (AUS)

Pferdemenges, Petra (G)   Higgs, Alan (UK)
McGlade, John (AUS)   McAdam, James (UK)
Neille, Stephen (AUS)   Kalinina, Tanya (UK)
Saunt, Deborah (UK)   Greer, Timothy (AUS)
Snooks, Roland (AUS)   Tonkin, Peter (AUS)
Wilkins, Gretchen (USA)   Boyarsky, Nicholas
Brown, John (CDN)   Brew, Peter (AUS)
Watson, Fleur (AUS)   Joris, Ephraim (B)
Banney, Michael (AUS)   Pendal, Simon (AUS)
Kahn, Jaffer (India)   Twose, Simon (NZ)
Winkler, Belinda (AUS)   Kebbel, Samuel
Simeoni, Robert (AUS)   Bruhn, Cameron (AUS)
Lyon, Carey (AUS)   Reed, Toby (AUS)
Lyon, Corbett (AUS)   Lavery, Michael (AUS)
Ni Einagh, Siobhan (IR)   Andrasek, Alisa (UK)

The core elements of the process remain as captured in this and previous editions of what has come to be known as The Pink Book, and it is the current practice for researchers in this program to situate research with reference to the key essay and the interviews here reprinted.

Reference may also be made to The Black Book and The Red Book, published by ACTAR alongside this volume: these feature many of the PhDs listed above.

We note that Richard Blythe, formerly Dean of the School of Architecture and Design at RMIT, co-initiator the ADAPTR grant and initiator of the OLT grant has moved on to Virginia Tech; we note with great sadness the untimely passing of Dr Johan Verbeke, the co-initator of the ADAPTr grant; the earlier passing of Randolph Glanville who introduced the research program to St Lucas, and the equally sudden passing of Dr Lucas Devriendt who we knew as an exemplary reflective practitioner of Art whose progress through the various Practice Research Symposia during his research inspired us all.

Leon van Schaik AO
RMIT, Melbourne.

INTRODUCTIONS

IN PRACTICE—RESEARCH CASE STUDIES

TABLE OF CONTENTS

COMPLETION SEMINARS

ON REFLECTION—THE PRACTICE RESEARCH SYMPOSIUM

Professor Kate Heron is Head, School of Architecture, Westminster University London and Principal of award-winning and widely published Feary + Heron Architects.

I have been a participant in the Invitational Design Practice Research Program at RMIT both as examiner of completed PhD and Master's candidates, and as a panel member at interim design crits. I continue to be in the thrall of the Research Symposium, this inventive device that enables practitioners to evolve in their practice through their own self-interrogation and re-discovery. I watch and contribute to the growth of this community of knowledge that develops and grows in its maturity, and welcome the new generation of participants emerging Europe-wide.

It is obvious that architecture is multi-diverse and worldwide – a global cultural endeavour. It follows that there are innumerable approaches to its related theory and teaching. It is less obvious that practitioners in one patch engage with practices in another patch, other than in manners akin to cultural imperialism. Too often, such engagement seems to be protective and self-referential. So the Research Symposia, using the activity of practice, could provide rich common ground and life-enhancing individual development.

At each Research Symposium I am struck by the extraordinary generosity of participants – by their openness, by their willingness to engage in peer review, and by their understanding that peer review is essential, and that practices who might be competitors in the ruthlessly competitive job market are willing to work together for the advancement of collective knowledge through practice.

Melbourne has enjoyed the benefit of this process over more than twenty years, and the effect on the city and beyond is widely applauded as being due to the individual and brilliant focus accorded it by Leon van Schaik. But is has moved beyond one person, and has itself evolved a worldwide influence. The scrutiny and rigour of the nature of practice is drawn back into the academy for these moments, but its base is in the world of practice and practitioners. Just as the work of an artist may be disseminated in a public showing or performance, the research laboratory is firmly based in the workshop or studio. So the dissemination of architects' work may be in buildings or published projects, but the laboratory for invention is in its own practice and engagement with peer review.

LI SHIQIAO

Li Shiqiao is the Weedon Professor in Asian Architecture at Virginia University. His research is concerned with understanding emergent conditions in Chinese cities by contextualising them in traditional discourses of modernity and architecture in Western and Asian manifestations.

The rise of data and the decline of moralised proportion since the seventeenth century have reconstituted the architectural profession in profound ways. The full impact of this reconstitution emerged in recent decades in architectural education: data cultivates its own ideal human being in the form of the specialist, whose expertise fulfils more effectively the demands of data-driven accounting methods used in tenure and promotion systems in universities, Research Assessment Exercises linked to funding, and commodification of knowledge and regulations in universities simulating market forces. Data does not seem to have a capacity to categorise acts of design – the work of the master-architect – and therefore neglects its crucial role in society. The phenomenon of 'design practice research' at RMIT since 1987, in this context, is historically important; it brings the importance of the 'mastery' of the master-architect back to the centre of design research. Mastery is infinitely more complex than specialist knowledge; it is the groundbreaking achievement of the RMIT design practice research program to root the notion of design innovation in the act, and to build the knowledge of design so that it is not exclusively in the forms of historicisation, systemisation, psychologisation and contextualisation of design. The act of design is where innovation is sorely needed: all social, political and academic work, if they care about design at all, must be centred on the act of design. It is perhaps no longer conceivable to re-moralise proportion, but it is possible and indeed desirable to re-conceptualise data. Instead of giving rise to the parametric as a caricature of design, data should foreground technicity as evidence of mastery. This extraordinary volume cements the pioneer status of the RMIT design practice research program; it incites a reformation of architecture that is critically important in the age of data.

Professor of Architecture
Innovation Chair
School of Architecture and
Design RMIT

This book marks the twenty-fifth anniversary of the initiation of the design practice research program at RMIT. This program, known as the 'Invitational Program', stemmed from an invitation to architects to reflect on their mastery of their discipline as demonstrated in a body of work acclaimed by their peers in awards, reviews and exhibition. It also marks the maturing of this research mode in the establishment of the program in Europe and in South-East Asia. The book commences with my personal account of the research program, its purposes and its practices, recalling how it came into being, and how it has developed into its currently prevailing form. There is a focus on the Research Symposium, the biannual forum that drives the design practice research program. Using the research completion dates, a chronologically ordered set of case studies of a sample of researchers, conducted by Anna Johnson, follows. A review of the contributions of the chief architects of the program concludes Anna Johnson's case studies. This is followed by extracts from the Plenary Sessions that conclude all Research Symposia. These give a glimpse of the engagement with the program of critics and practitioners from all over the world. Professor Richard Blythe then concludes with an account of the progress of his internationalising strategy for the program. The Forewords by Professor Kate Heron and Professor Li Shiqiao set the scene, and in the Postscript Professor Johan Verbeke describes how he came to learn about the program, investigated it and then invited the program to operate under his institution's auspices in Belgium.

Leon van Schaik
Melbourne
October 2011

LEON VAN SCHAIK

The Evolution of the Invitational Program in Design Practice Research

The Invitational Program was preceded by the ambition to conduct research in the medium of architectural design practice *(i)*. It was propelled by curiosity about the 'natural history of creative practitioners' *(ii)*. This in turn was impelled by research into the ways in which architects construct their mental space using their spatial intelligence *(iii)*. The approach thus invited practitioners to look back, to observe current practice and to project forward into future practice (also described as a scholarship cone, the base of which was previous practice, the middle of which was current practice, and the tip of which pointed to future practice) *(iv)*. Through this research we have discovered that in this domain as in others, architects achieving intellectual change work 'enchained' to mentors, peers and challengers in three polar clusters *(v)*. The workings of these relationships constitute the 'public behaviours' that sustain venturous design practice. Our 'research in the medium' goal is now also pursued through a 'by publication' process of capturing the processes of design practice *(vi)*.

WHAT IS THE INVITATIONAL PROGRAM OF DESIGN PRACTICE RESEARCH?

Design Practice Research at RMIT began in the late 1980s when, recently arrived in Melbourne and enthralled by its architecture, I invited practitioners to join me in examining the nature of the mastery demonstrated in a body of their work that had already been acclaimed through awards, exhibition, publication and/or other peer review. Then, I argued, they could examine their current projects in the light of this new or refreshed understanding, and – after this reflection – speculate in the medium of design about possible futures for their practice. This invitation – now open because, through word of mouth, many invite themselves – has resulted in a research program that has involved more than one hundred practitioners from three continents. Honouring its beginnings, the research program is known as 'the Invitational Program'. It commenced as a research Master's; it now operates at Doctoral level in a two modes: one emphasising the investigation into the nature of mastery (PhD 'by project'), the other focusing on the surfacing of evidence about internationally acclaimed mastery (PhD 'by publication'). The format of the research program is structured by biannual[1] symposia known as Research Symposia.

What we learned from the first fifteen years was documented in the book *Mastering Architecture* (2005), subject of the second RIBA Research Symposium

---

1   Initially in 1988 there were three Research Symposia per annum, but this proved to be out of step with the work rhythms of candidates who are overwhelmingly established in practice and conducting practice-based research.

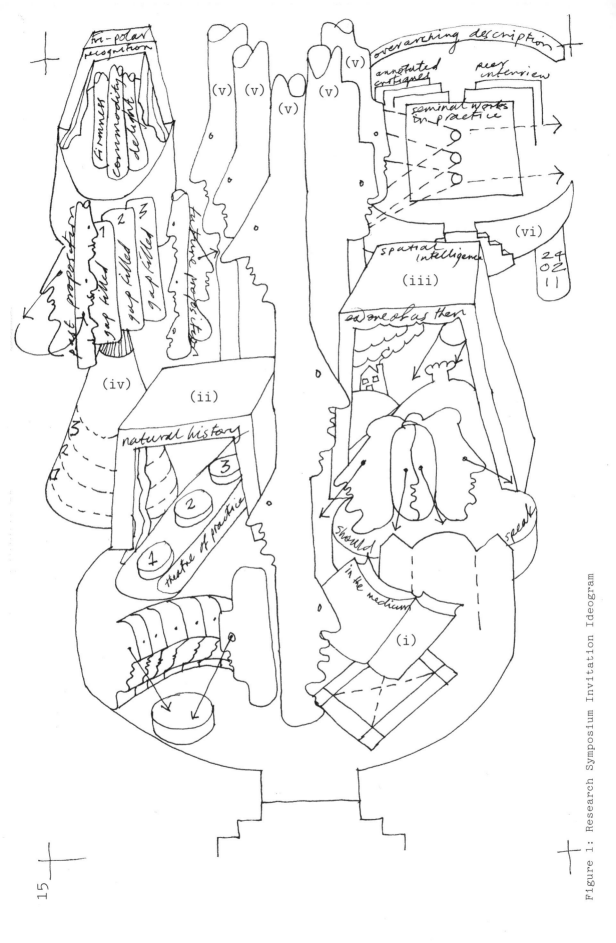

Figure 1: Research Symposium Invitation Ideogram

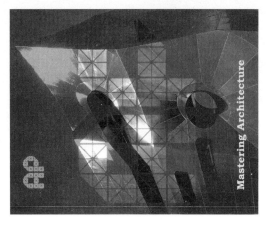

Figure 2: Cover of *Mastering Architecture*

on 19 September 2007.[2] ,The modes of engagement are summarised in an ideogram (see figure 3, opposite).

This ideogram summarises concerns and processes of the Invitational Program in a shoebox theatre. The invitation creates the proscenium arch; the curtains frame up the action with research into creative practice; the rear of the stage lists background concepts, and the cube presents a 'natural history of creative practitioners'-face *(Y)*, a 'public behaviours of creative practice'-face *(Z)* and an 'integrated scholarship'-face *(X)*. Practices roll past this onto the stage where their individual investigations play out. The profiles in the foreground signal the ways in which we observe through our 'enchainments' – those links in our spatial and relational histories.

One facet of the central cube in this concerns the natural history of the innovative architect; another covers the *'public'*[3] *or group behaviours that sustain or thwart mastery. The third visible face joins these with the concept of 'integrated scholarship'*. In these fields of practice the current positions of participating practitioners are interrogated through a meticulous uncovering of their *'enchainments'*.[4] The linked histories in space that have forged their *'mental space'*[5] are investigated, as are the educational experiences that have transformed these. The research reveals the web of mentors, worthy adversaries, peers and challengers within which designers work.

THE RESEARCH SYMPOSIUM IS THE PUBLIC BEHAVIOUR OF THE INVITATIONAL PROGRAM

The second face of the Research Symposium 'cube' pictured in Figure 3 covers public behaviours. Much of what has been discovered about innovative design practice through the investigations of the Invitational stream concerns the building of what might be termed 'the brain of the firm'[6] – its enchainments, its social system, the sum of the public behaviours that shape its design practice. The growth of this understanding has been paralleled by the slow evolution of the Research Symposium as the principal public behaviour of this design practice mode of research. Although at the outset we attempted three Research

2   'Reflective Research: Mastering Architecture and Creative Innovation', RIBA Research Symposium, 19 September 2007, London.

3   The term comes from Randall Collins. Collins, R 2000, *The sociology of philosophies: a global theory of intellectual change*, Harvard University Press, Camb., Mass. pp. 42, 380, 879-881.

4   Ibid.

5   Schaik, L van 2008, *Spatial intelligence: new futures for architecture*, John Wiley & Sons, Chichester, pp. 40-42.

6   Stafford Beer, A 1972, *Brain of the firm*, The Professional Library, Penguin Books, London.

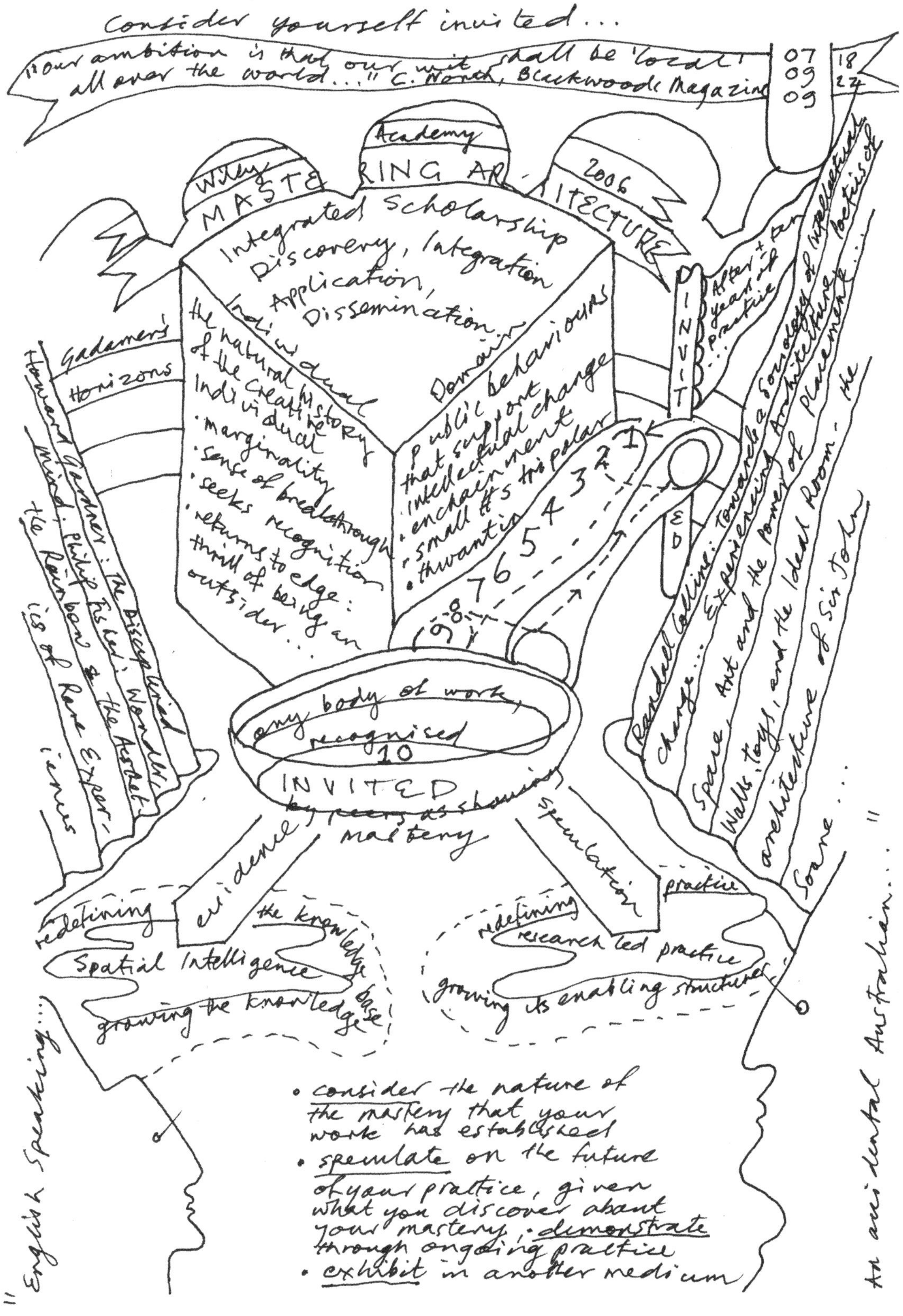

Figure 3: The Invitational Cube

Symposia in the year, today the Research Symposium is a twice-yearly gathering of research candidates enrolled at RMIT in disciplines associated with architecture and design. The Research Symposium's prime purpose is to be the tangible focus of a learning community – its home, so to speak. As we all know, people learn more from each other than they do from abstract structures at breakfast, at tea and coffee breaks, over lunch, at pre-lecture drinks, at the Research Symposium banquets, and in the restaurants and bars of the host cities: Melbourne and, since 2009, Ghent. The Research Symposium is thus crucially a gathering of peers.

In addition to being a long weekend of formal and informal peer review of research in progress, the Research Symposium brings together these candidates with visiting critics from around Australia and from all over the world. We aim to invite critics who are emerging onto the scene, and many names that are now very familiar in the fields of design have been critics here in the decades since the first Research Symposium. The weekend commences with public lectures by visiting critics who are new to the Research Symposia or by award-winning, completed PhD candidates. This is followed by a social occasion, a banquet or a barbecue, and it proceeds with two days of work-in-progress reviews. There are potentially almost two hundred people involved in any Research Symposium, and reviews in Melbourne now run in up to ten parallel streams, while in Ghent there are already two.

The secondary purpose of the Research Symposium is to structure the work of supervisors and their research candidates. Twice a year candidates are asked to present their work-in-progress to panels, and these presentations are organically related to everyone's research work plans. Typically the initial Research Symposium presentation scopes the propositions arising from the candidate's review of past work; the second Research Symposium provides through project and literature reviews a survey of the enchainments in which that work was conducted; a series of intermediate Research Symposia cover tranches of project work devised to address research gaps identified between proposition and review; and in a penultimate Research Symposium – prior to their completion seminar at a final Research Symposium – candidates present the outlines of their catalogues, research catalogue, or *durable visual records* together with their design for their final presentation through exhibition, web, film or performance.

Candidates present to panels made up of supervisors and external critics, but sessions are open to all, and all attending are invited to enter into the proceedings. Candidates present their work for up to half an hour, and in the remaining half-hour chairs of panels construct around that work the best possible conversation: a conversation that aims to help the candidate further their work. Examination is by viva, and the format is not dissimilar to that of the panels of the Research Symposium. A chairperson, who is a research candidate supervisor but not the candidate's supervisor, convenes a panel of three examiners selected by the supervisor and endorsed by the Head of School and RMIT's Higher Degrees Committee. The candidate presents to this panel in open public session, using an exhibition or equivalent to support that presentation. These events are better understood as 'completion seminars' because the conversations with the candidates always result in further refinements of the research dissemination. Video recordings are made to capture the exhibition, the presentation and the discussion, and these recordings form part of the archived durable visual record. We also use these for the guidance of commencing candidates, and for quality assurance purposes. They take place in the week before the work-in-progress weekends, and the work remains on public view for that week. Over a long weekend, therefore, any candidate can experience every stage of the process from commencement to conclusion, and they can do so across a wide range of domains.

The weekend concludes with a plenary session in which candidates, stream co-ordinators and visitors are invited to comment on proceedings and to give advice on how to improve the event. This plenary session drives to the final aim of the Research Symposium – that they should embed, also organically, the memory of the community of learning and its growing cultural capital. Examples of the feedback, endorsing the approach and suggesting refinements, are given in the Research Symposium Plenary section at the end of this book.

WHAT LAY BEHIND THE INITIATION OF THIS PROGRAM?

When I arrived in Australia for the first time in 1986 as prospective Head of Architecture at RMIT, I was taken on drives around Melbourne to see the significant new work in the city, work I had been alerted to by Rory Spence's article in Architectural Review.[7] It took a day to visit three projects. Significant though this work was, it was clearly peripheral in Melbourne, at least in a geographical sense. I soon became aware that it was peripheral in a cultural sense too, because while there already existed – as Spence wrote – important organs for building the local culture of architecture, notably Transition (a self-proclaimed 'Journal of Architectural Discourse') and the Half Time Club (a forum for beginning practitioners), the gala events around which the culture gyrated were visits by architectural stars from the northern hemisphere. Being peripheral to the city was one thing, but the attitude of being *peripheral to the world* was even more pervasive. I discovered on my return to the north that the innovative work that I had seen was indeed – as the Melburnians I had met feared – patronisingly dismissed as a dim resonance of what was already happening elsewhere (probably on the west coast of the USA, Europeans would say). Perhaps because I am – even with my northern sensibilities – at core a southerner, I resented this, and determined to do something about it. In 1987 and 1988 I called several meetings of practitioners recognised as creative innovators in the local culture and challenged them to research the nature of their innovation. This research, I argued, would capture evidence about the nature of the mastery that their work displayed, reveal its local authenticity, and equip them to take part in the discourses that nourished the 'stars' that they so avidly sought out and brought south to worship in massed assemblies. I confess that I taunted them about this one-way transmission of architectural knowledge from

7   Spence, R 1985, 'Australia Sydney/Melbourne', in P Davey (ed.), *Architectural Review*, The Architectural Press, London.

northern metropoles to a (self-defined) peripheral province, noting that they were not being invited back into the world despite their fêting of the visitors.

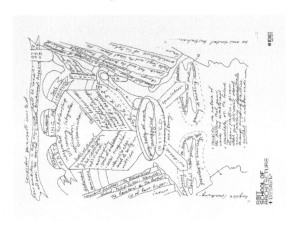

Figure 4: The Invitational Ideogram as in the Research Symposium EU Poster

I had another motive, and that was to inculcate an approach to research that was not 'about' design, but that was *research in the medium of design itself*. So it was that the challenge issued to these architects was: "Come back into the critical frame of the school of architecture and examine the nature of the mastery that you are acknowledged to have achieved. Describe the architectural nature of that mastery; speculate on the future of your practice in the light of this reflection, and conduct that speculation through the medium of design and in the context of the ongoing work of your practice. Present that evidence and your speculation in a form other than the work itself, and condense your findings into an exhibition no larger than three containers 500 x 1200 x 1500 millimetres[8] and a twenty-four-page catalogue."

Having emerged from fifteen years of practice, I knew that to have a chance of success the research work plan had to dovetail with the exigencies of practice. It had to have precise constraints and determined deadlines. At best it would be run as a project in the office of the practitioner. The initial review stage worked in with office archiving and advertising needs, the speculation about the future began with examining the impact of the research on work ongoing, and the outcomes were tightly defined and related to a specified set of progress reports – made through a regular meeting of the candidates in a practice Research Symposium.

HOW DID THE RESEARCH SYMPOSIUM DEVELOP?

It was very important for the gravitas of the enterprise at the pioneering stage to have well-known international critics at these sessions, and Michael Sorkin, Mario Gandelsonas, Diane Agrest, Beatrice Colomina and Mark Wigley were among the earliest to oblige. At that stage, thanks to my practice background combined with a Doctorate about that practice, I was the only one amongst my colleagues qualified to supervise the first cohorts of invited candidates. I realised that I needed to create a system of mutual support amongst them. This was the origin of the Research Symposium: we arranged that regular

8   At this stage we anticipated using unlet office floors in the city as the venue for the exhibitions, and we constructed boxes of this dimension to house the exhibits. From the outset, the architects found ways of creatively subverting and transcending this framework.

work-in-progress presentations would be made to the entire group, and the presentations were open to their peers at large, and to undergraduates. In time we added firstly an Urban Architecture stream to enable recent graduates to build up a body of work demonstrating mastery, a stream that is today the Urban Architecture Laboratory. Later this initiatory level was added to by an Embedded Practice stream, in which recent graduates were hosted by practices and SIAL (the Spatial Information Architecture Laboratory at RMIT) as they established a practice position in the realm of parametric design. Streams grew to include Landscape Architecture, Interior Design, Industrial Design, Fashion and the History and Theory of Practice. For some years, the Research Symposium hosted a Media and Communications stream; many of those associated with this are now at Parsons The New School for Design in New York.

The earliest attempt to internationalise the program occurred in Singapore between 1994 and 2000. Six notable emerging practitioners[9] identified by William Lim joined the program after a series of presentations about the approach. Here in 1995 Ignasi de Solà-Morales made his famous comment about architecture in a diaspora, observing that in its need to indicate its knowledge of the world at large it displayed a "pornography of modernism". These practitioners have gone on to become the most awarded group of architects in the region. We still only had one possible supervisor in the program, and it was impossible to devote the energy needed to identify and bring on a second generation. A subsequent attempt to internationalise through the University of Westminster, where I became a visiting professor (2004), foundered when the then-Dean dismissed the enthusiastic advocacy of Head of School, Kate Heron, saying to us: "We send ideas to the colonies, we don't import them!" More recently since 2009 (with a few trials in Brussels in the previous three years), the Invitational Program has operated in Ghent (directed by Martyn Hook of RMIT and hosted by the Sint-Lucas School of Architecture). This time, internationalisation is working because the RIBA Seminar created a broad awareness of the model; because there is a perceived need within European institutions, many of which have been grappling with how to undertake design practice research; and because at RMIT we now have a complete generation of practitioner academics who have completed the program and who are in a position to supervise candidates. Observers from Sint-Lucas, Aarhus and the Macintosh have attended Research Symposia in Melbourne with a view to engaging with the RMIT model. There are already in excess of twenty European practices engaged in the program through Ghent, with interest spreading fast. And finally, internationalisation of the program in the interests of building a broad acceptance of the approach is a key School strategic objective, allied to RMIT University's stated aim to be a global university. Meanwhile, in Melbourne, over 100 practices have completed the Invitational Program since its inception in 1987, with the first cohort completing in 1991. More than 30 are currently engaged in Invitational research.

9   Mok Wei Wei, Look Boon Gee, Richard Hassell (with the active support of his partner Mun Sum Wong), Frank Ling and Richard Ho.

The platform on which the Invitational Program sits is constructed from a few basic ideas.

```
FOUNDATION IDEAS (1):
MENTAL SPACE
```

Coming from the southern hemisphere in my early teens, I encountered northern spatiality as palpably alien and therefore as an observably constructed system. In my Architectural Association Diploma dissertation I argued that it was imperative that those designing spaces should be aware of their own histories in space and the mental space that they had constructed from that history. Invited practitioners are challenged to become aware of their mental space – an argument fully developed in the book *Spatial Intelligence*.

Figure 5: *Spatial Intelligence* Book Cover

This ideogram is based on a shoebox theatre. We are the audience, and the profiles on the lower-left and along the right-hand-side represent some of that audience. People are there to remind us that everyone has a personal history in space, built up around our spatial intelligence. Some profiles contain key points about spatial intelligence. The curtains to the left list other human intelligences and note that our intelligence is emotionally framed, and inflected by our relationships. The right-hand curtains note the evolution of our spatial intelligence over millennia, and cite WG Sebald as a writer who describes life through space. The proscenium arch notes, "Design City Melbourne: the mental space of the city is housed in its great works of architecture…" Drops note the search for continuums in human experience of space: domestic to professional, and the phenomenon of 'relegation to the humdrum' that erodes our spatial awareness in everyday life. On the stage, a banner quotes Gaston Bachelard's *Poetics of Space*: "the house holds childhood motionless in its arms." Below this, on the stage, two personae watch a spatial tennis game…while in front of them a spiral of spatial engagement twirls, the first-order awareness of the surveyor followed by the lawyer, then the engineer, and now the second-order awareness of the architect. Each side of the stair are mnemonics for spatial analyses of spaces domestic and workaday. (*Spatial Intelligence*, p.13)

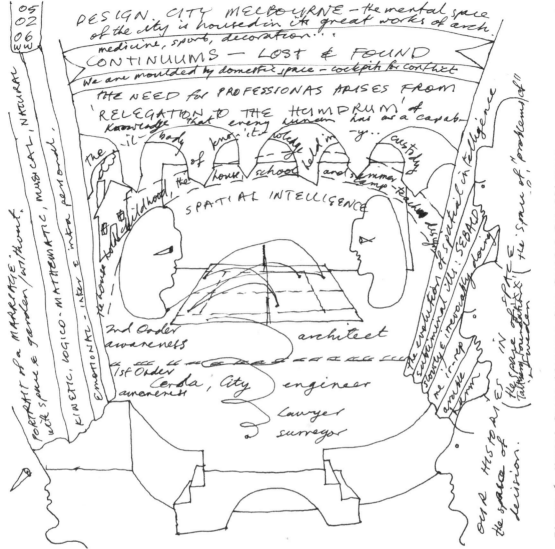

FOUNDATION IDEAS (2):
RESEARCH IN THE MEDIUM OF DESIGN ITSELF

While teaching at the Architectural Association in the 1970s I became very concerned that, while an architect like Sir John Soane was greatly studied and written about, no-one was addressing what he actually did architecturally. The effect of this is demonstrated when you examine what people who claim to be influenced by him have done in his name, be they Gwathmey, Venturi Scott Brown or Johnson. The idea of a house-museum flows across, but the architectural ideas do not. I was determined that what we should research was the architectural production of architects, and that we should do this through their architecture: in the medium itself.

Out of this came the slogan: Research in the Medium Itself. This signalled a determination to investigate architecture through architecture and not through history or theory, social or environmental science though – as

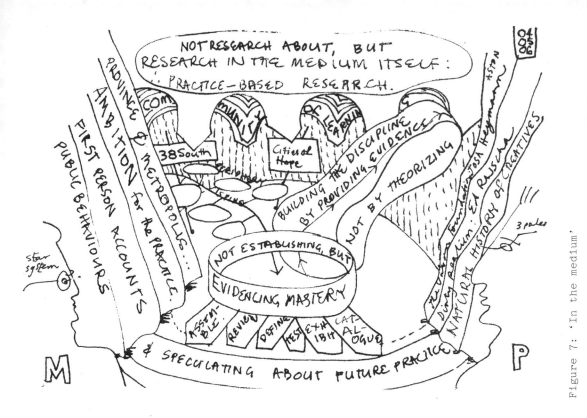

Figure 7: 'In the medium'

with Reyner Banham's *Well Tempered Environment*[10] (environmental science) or Tafuri[11] (socio-political analysis) or Blau[12] and Guttmann[13] (sociology of practice) – I certainly valued work in those arenas, and still do. And some of my self-enchained mentors, Venturi[14] or Scott Brown and Venturi[15] for example, or Rem Koolhaas,[16] were already engaged in research in the medium itself, although generalised outside their own practice.

FOUNDATION IDEAS (3):
DIRECT ENGAGEMENT OF PRACTITIONERS

The next idea concerned intermediaries – or rather, how to avoid them. Working with urbanising communities in southern Africa, I observed how mediating figures blocked the connections between designers and those they were designing for. This 'blocking' was well meaning, but destroyed the possibility of fresh architectural insight into the issues facing people. Again the problem was

10 Banham, R 1973, *The architecture of the well-tempered environment*, The Architectural Press, London [first published 1960].

11 Tafuri, M 1976, *Architecture and utopia: design and capitalist development*, MIT Press, Camb., Mass.

12 Blau, JR 1987, *Architects and firms: a sociological perspective on architectural practices*, MIT Press, Camb., Mass.

13 Gutman R 1988, *Architectural practice: a critical view*, Princeton Architectural Press, Princeton.

14 Venturi, R 1968, *Complexity and contradiction in architecture*, MOMA, New York.

15 Scott Brown, D and Venturi, R 1972, *Learning from Las Vegas*, MIT Press, Camb., Mass.

16 Koolhaas, R 1994, *Delirious New York: a retroactive manifesto for Manhattan*, Monacelli Press, New York [first published 1978].

in the translation of architectural need or intent into words: a failure to work in the medium itself.

As a practitioner academic since graduating from the Architectural Association School in 1971, I have become very aware that the research focus of a school comes to lead the studio practice: our research focus predisposes us to see ways of doing things that align with our research approach. A snapshot of the graduation exhibitions of three London schools illustrates this (Fig. 8): in 2006, the AA show consisted almost entirely of algorithmic caves echoing the research of the Design Research Unit at that school, while the Bartlett show presented arrays of virtuoso illustrations of esoteric architectural ideas in a seeming response to the cultural studies focus of its research, while at Westminster the focus on reflective practice ensured that both of these poles and a more pragmatic project orientation were equally present.

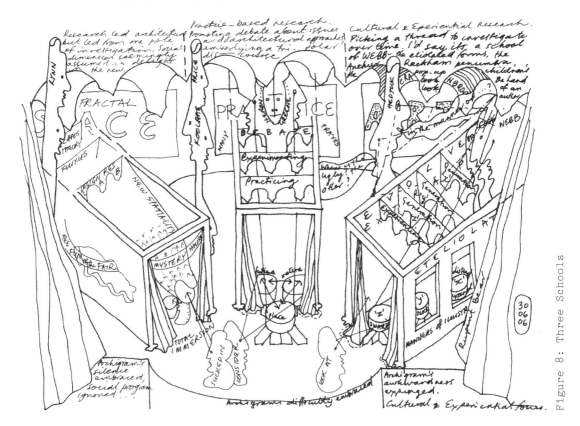

Figure 8: Three Schools

What has also become evident to me as an educator is the debilitating effect of dualistic thinking on the relationship between schools and practice.[17]

17   Schaik, L van 2012, 'Modernism and contemporaneity in architecture: peripheries and centres', in SW William & JH Chang (eds), *Non-west modernist past: on architecture & modernities*, World Scientific Publishing Company, Singapore, pp. 47-58.

Research has come to be seen as something outside of practice, be it in the offices or in the academies. Ironically there is research that demonstrates the fatuity of this duality. Extensive analysis of academic practice – revealing what the professoriate in universities actually do, rather than what they say they do – led to the concept of 'integrated practice'.[18] The study revealed that practitioners do not research or teach; they engage in four closely interrelated modes of scholarship: Discovery, or the uncovering of new knowledge; Integration, or the incorporating of new knowledge into the existing knowledge base of a field; Application, or the establishing of ways in which to apply new or newly integrated knowledge into practice; and Dissemination, or the communicating of knowledge through publishing, lecturing and designing learning environments. These scholarships – as our Invitational Program has demonstrated – flow through the practice of architecture, and through what we do in schools – the latter acknowledged by the researchers who found that integrated scholarship was most unabashedly observable at work in schools of architecture. The concept is critical to helping practitioners observe and understand their own practice. 'Research', however, still seems to far too many to be something necessarily done in a medium different from their design practice and in a place other than where they practice.

FOUNDATION IDEAS (5):
PUBLIC BEHAVIOURS: RECOGNITION

As a practitioner, I had been puzzled about how to seek recognition for my own work, carried out in marginal or exceptional circumstances[19] and requiring – as so much work outside the mainstream does – particular forums for meaningful critique. As a practitioner, churning out work, you seek out recognition but most forums that might address what you are trying to do are predicated on other concerns. And few editors have a vision that extends beyond the immediately apparent novelty. How, then, do you identify who is working in your arena? In time this line of enquiry led me to an understanding of how the ancient triad of architectural values – Firmness, Commodity and Delight[20] – form separate poles of architectural endeavour, each causing a distinctive mode of practice. We all privilege one of these poles over the others, even as we seek to satisfy them all. Thus we create different practices. And applying ourselves to architecture in particular places produces results that are necessarily of their province (that place where our mental space and that of our clients engage); even if our work is not thus 'provincial' in the sense that the work cannot be appreciated out of its context.[21] Nonetheless, seeking recognition propels us out

18   Boyer, EL 1990, *Scholarship reconsidered: priorities of the professoriate*, The Carnegie Foundation for the Advancement of Teaching, Princeton, NJ.

19   Marginal: alts and adds, exceptional working in slums

20   The triad aligning comfortably with the driving dynamic of creativity uncovered by Randall Collins in his investigation into the sociology of intellectual change.

21   O'Doherty, B 1986, *Inside the white cube: the ideology of the gallery space*, University of California Press, Berkeley and Los Angeles, p. 79.

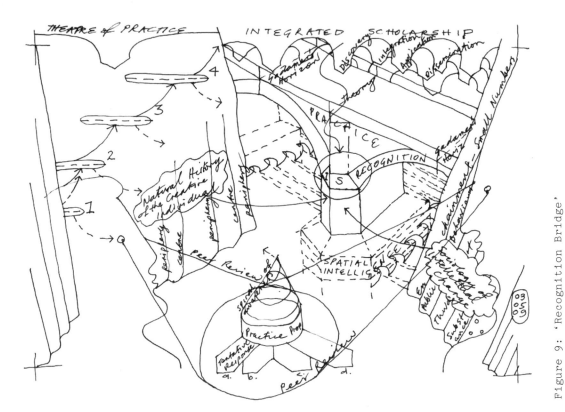

of our provinces and enriches our enchainments. If we are canny, as we seek the best possible conversation about our work, we forge a metropolis around our work. The successful creative careers we have studied through the work of our invited practitioners demonstrate many ways of building forums that deliver firm yet benevolent critique.

THE METHOD: FROM MASTER'S TO PHD

So it is that when I began to work with the practitioners in Melbourne, the model for the research was one that involved looking back over a body of work that had received critical acclaim, and investigating its architectural ideas and their spatial and intellectual enchainments. These were uncovered by relating the works to the formation of the practitioner's mental space;[22] locating designed projects relative to past and current trajectories in the evolution of the architect's 'natural history' as a creative practitioner, and relating them to emerging recognition structures. This exploration was conducted in the presence of peers. It was followed by a period in which current projects were closely observed in the light of the earlier forensics. And the process concluded in speculations about future practice conducted through emerging design projects.

Over the years, this initial model evolved to encompass PhD-level research into the nature of the mastery evidenced in a body of work. This was, however – as exemplified in the PhDs of Shane Murray, Jenny Lowe and SueAnne Ware – constructed on the same basic method. Observe and analyse a body of work. Derive from this a clear understanding of the (provincial)

22   Schaik, L van 2008, *Spatial intelligence: new futures for architecture*, John Wiley & Sons, Chichester.

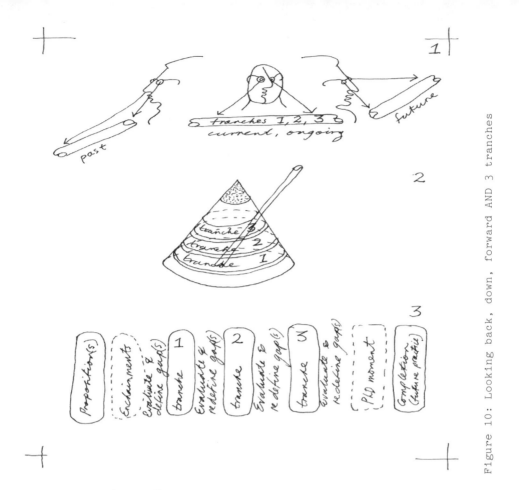

1   The research involves investigating enchainments by looking
     back, by looking at current work in progress, and by speculating
     about future practice.
2   The cone of research: at the base the existing body of work,
     above it tranches of work conducted in the light of examining
     the mastery of that work, and a concluding tranche speculating
     on future practice.
3   The cone seen as a bar chart.

architectural intentions of the work, and of how that work is situated within
its national and international (metropolitan) context, thus defining the
community of learning capable of engaging it in its best possible metropolitan
conversation.[23] Identify the propositions driving your design practice, and
analyse the gaps between where you (and your peers) are on the path to a
fulfilment of those propositions. Conduct the next tranche of your work in
the light of that analysis. Evaluate and redefine the gaps. Conduct another
tranche of work. Evaluate and redefine the gaps. Conduct a closing tranche of
work in the light of this redefinition. (In the Master's, there was one tranche
of work.) Conclude by speculating through design on possible future practices

23   See: Schaik, L van 1987, 'Province and Metropolis', *AA Files*,
      Architectural Association, No. 14, pp. 48-54.
      See also: Schaik, L van 1996, 'Province and Metropolis', in
      Middleton, R (ed.), *Architectural associations: the idea of the city*,
      Architectural Association, London, pp. 156-178.

ensuing from this investigation. Consistently this model has revealed hitherto undocumented design practice processes, unmasking intuition and making a major contribution to knowledge in the domain.

DIFFERENT PHD MODES SUIT PRACTITIONERS AT DIFFERENT STAGES OF THEIR CAREERS

We now observe differing PhD modes at play in our postgraduate research. There is a small stream pursuing the history and theory of design practice, aiming for new contributions to historical and/or theoretical knowledge about design. The research is conducted in accord with the norms of the scholarly excellence for written work. These PhDs are examined 'by thesis', in that a printed thesis is sent away to three external examiners for evaluation. This thesis is the sole component evaluated.

Crossing all disciplinary streams except the Invitational is an approach that attracts practitioners setting out on their careers and seeking to discover further rationales for their practice approach. They produce new knowledge about design by scoping and testing through design key propositions that they believe may influence practice. A body of work is produced. These PhDs are examined according to RMIT's regulations for 'by project' research (as below). This accounts for about one-third of the research conducted.

The Invitational Program aims to produce new knowledge from existing practice by deriving propositions from that practice, comparing these to those that can be discerned in aligned practices elsewhere, and surfacing the processes of design practice. These PhDs are examined according to RMIT's 'by project' regulations: an appropriate durable record is created and supplied to a panel of three external examiners six weeks prior to a viva. An hour-long presentation is made to that panel in the context of an exhibition event that further delineates the research into design processes. The evaluation covers three components: the durable record, the exhibition event and the viva.

Research in the Invitational Program can be conducted through RMIT's 'by publication' regulations, where the PhD involves documenting in an appropriate archival form a range of seminal, internationally recognised projects; interacting with some respected critics in the field; and speculating through design (presented in an exhibition) about the impact of the research on future practice. The 'by project' modes for practitioner reflection on, or establishment of, a body of work account for almost two-thirds of the research conducted through the RMIT Research Symposia.[24]

24   The proportions vary slightly from Research Symposium to Research Symposium. In the June 2010 Research Symposium, the ratios of the above (taken from candidate abstracts and completions) were:

Master's:
· New Practitioner (18/22) 82%
· Invited Practitioner (4/22) 18%

PhD:
· History and Theory (10/70) 14% (unusually high)
· New Practitioner (22/70) 31%
· Invited Practitioner (39/70) 55%

(Leon van Schaik, 31 May 2010)

The recasting of the 'Invitational' stream as a PhD 'by publication' restores the primacy of design practice in the research. Something of the immediacy of working in the medium of design itself had dissipated as the shift from a research Master's to a PhD occurred. Despite our stated intentions, the burden of the research catalogue had fallen increasingly on text. To counter this we might have maintained the Master's-level investigation, but have decided not to follow this path for two chief reasons. The first is one of equity. Many of the Master's-level researches nudge close to PhDs in extent and scope. This is clearly unfair. The other is the general adoption of the Bologna Accord and the disappearance of the Master's by Research as an understandable entity, when the vast preponderance of Master's awarded around the world are by coursework.

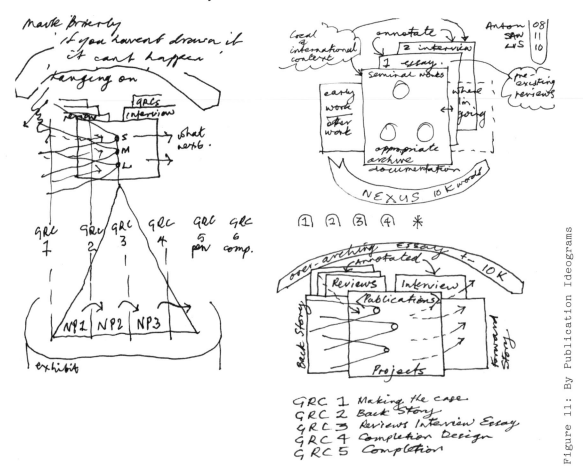

Figure 11: By Publication Ideograms

These ideograms document the evolution of the model as senior supervisor Prof. SueAnne Ware and second supervisor Prof. Leon van Schaik worked with Landscape Architects Kevin Taylor, Kate Cullity and Perry Lethlean as they plotted their research process in the Invitational Program. The central square in these ideograms contains the seminal projects that have been 'published' – that is, designed and published or constructed. They trail cones to the left, the 'back story': discursive accounts of how these projects evolved. Stacked behind these are arrays of published reviews – collected, analysed and annotated by the designer. Arrows pointing to the right project a 'forward story': a speculation about future practice. Behind this, and impelling it, is an in-depth interview by a respected critic, transcribed, referenced and illustrated and developed as a scholarly document. The banner above represents the researcher's overarching account of the scholarship of the PhD.

How to bring the architecture itself back into the core of PhD-level research by invited candidates became an urgent issue for us. Calling on Dr Nikos Papastergiadis – long-time adviser to me on the evolution of the PhD program – I proposed that we treat the Invitational Program as a PhD 'by publication' in which the publications are built (or designed) projects that have received the admiration of peers and other critical attention, locally and internationally. This is the model we now use. Candidates continue to be 'selected' because they have an appropriate body of work. They examine that work critically in order to identify seminal projects and design processes that have impelled their practice. They document their seminal projects to an appropriate archival standard. They assemble a fulsome bibliography of the critical attention the work has received, and reflect upon that critique, annotating reviews with comments as to its accuracy and its helpfulness, or otherwise. A peer interview is arranged, in which the candidate is questioned about their findings by an informed and admired critic. This interview is edited to become a scholarly and generally accessible document, illustrated, annotated and fully referenced. These reflections contextualise the works, and provide evidence about the mental space in which they were conducted. The stages of this scholarship are presented in the usual way at Research Symposia. Typically two presentations are devoted to looking back; two to an explanation of what is seminal about the selected projects. The reflections on critique and on the interview are also presented at Research Symposia. At a penultimate Research Symposium, the candidate exposes the research in total, defines the overarching reflective essay that will capture the journey of the research and describes the exhibition event that will comprise the completion seminar for the PhD. In the usual way, these examinations are conducted through the Research Symposium.

The PhDs of Nigel Bertram and Paul Minifie have pioneered this approach, and the aim of foregrounding the actuality of the architecture itself was achieved to the satisfaction (with acclaim) of a panel of distinguished examiners from three continents. More importantly, these practitioners and the others who have undertaken the research report that their practice has been transformed for the better through the enhanced conscious understanding of their design processes. As Johan Van Den Berghe, a candidate nearing completion through the Research Symposium EU, said memorably in November 2010 as he revealed the results of an intensive investigation into his mental space enchainments: "You don't know what you know until you find it out!"

Invitational candidates have their research catalogues published. Six anthologies have been completed and more are planned (see Bibliography). Some of their vivas are viewable on:

`http://vimeo.com/21748481`

Figure 12: Publications

PHD CANDIDATES

NAME	DATE	TITLE OF DISSERTATION
Anderson, Benedict	2005	The architectural flaw: speculations on the reconstructed city
Anderson, Charles	2009	Ephemeral Architectures: towards a process architecture
Anderson, Lyndon	2001	Enrichment: a design strategy based upon observation
Bertram, Nigel	2010	Making and using the urban environment: furniture, structure, infrastructure
Black, Richard	2009	Site knowledge: in dynamic contexts
Blythe, Richard	2008	A terroir of TERROIR (or, a brief history of design-places)
Bremner, Craig	2001	New living models: design for the public image of home
Bruns, Antonia	2004	Spatial narrative in film, architecture and urban design
Collier, Stephen	2009	Paradigms of observation: azul oscuro casi negro: a blue that is almost black
Crist, Graham	2010	Sheds for Antarctica: the environment for architectural design and practice
Daniell, Thomas	2009	Negotiating context
Dodd, Melanie	2011	Between the lived and the built, foregrounding the user in design for the public realm
George, Beth	2009	Scouring the thin city: an investigation into Perth through the medium of mapping
Helsel, Sand	2009	A search for common pleasures: curating the city
Hogg, Geoff	2011	Repeatable shape: designing a cultural practice
Hook, Martyn	2008	The act of reflective practice: the emergence of Iredale Pedersen Hook Architects
Karakiwicz, Justyna	2002	Exploring the dimensions of urban densities
Krueger, Theodore III	2011	Designing Epistemology
Lee, Virginia	2006	The intention to notice: the collection, the tour and ordinary landscapes

Lim, Ngiom	2009	A structure for architectural innovation: mind-shaping
Lowe, Jennifer	2002	The space between: where dialogue takes place
Minifie, Paul	2010	Design domains: their relations and transformations as revealed through the practice of Paul Minifie
Mitsogianni, Vivian	2009	white noise PANORAMA: process based architectural design
Murray, Shane	2004	Architectural design and discourse
Neille, Stephen	2007	SPEED_SPACE: architecture, landscape and perceptual horizons
Reisner, Yael	2009	The troubled relationship between architecture and aesthetic: exploring the self and emotional beauty in design.
Trudgeon, Michael	2008	Zukunfstmusik: prototyping the technological and social construction of space
Ware, SueAnne	2005	Anti-memorials: rethinking the landscape of memory
Wicks, David	2010	Divining the structure: the use of graphic representation in the analysis and performance of dramatic material

MASTERS CANDIDATES

NAME	DATE	TITLE OF DISSERTATION
Balmforth, Scott	2007	TERROIR as a state of mind
Banney, Michael	2010	The Practice of m3architecture
Bruns, Antonia	1992	A+B=C: Film and Architecture: Narrative and Spatial Montage
Burne, Rosemary	2000	Baroque + Film <theory as>narrative/*.*:
Christensen, Michael	2010	The Practice of m3architecture
Cole, Sara	2005	Urban Moments
Craig, Thom	2002	Fine Films: layering personal visions in new places
Day, Norman	1994	Particular Architecture
Donovan, Brian	2004	DonovanHill: Strategies for delivering places that enable events
Eeckhout, Riet	2009	Design Armatures

EXAMINERS

Alter, Prof Kevin

Barker, Tom

Bremner, Craig

Brine, Dr. Judith

Burrry, Prof Mark

Carter, Paul

Colomina, Beatrice

Elliot, Peter

Engberg, Juliana

Findlay, Kathryn

Fournier, Colin

Fox, William L.

Li, Dr Shiqioa

London, Prof Geoffrey

Lyon, Carey

Maeseneer, Martine de

Massumi, Prof Brian

Mc Dougall, Ian

McBride, Rob

McQuire, Dr Scott

Mennan, Dr. Zeynep

Missingham, Greg

Munster, Anna

Neille, Stephen

Ostwald, Dr Micahel J

Papastergiadis, Dr Nikos

Porter, Prof David

Powell, Allan

Rashid, Hani

Scott, Dr Felicity

Sola-Morales, Prof Ignasi

Sorkin, Michael

Suzuki, Akira

Thompson, Kerstin

Till, Prof Jeremy

Treadwell, Sarah

Tsukamoto, Yoshihari

Van der Velde, Rene

Verbeke, Dr Johan

Walker, Linda Marie

Werrick, James

Wigley, Mark

Wright, David

Yeang, Dr Ken

RICHARD BLYTHE

"Thinking about Architecture, Thinking about Architects." 2000–2008 Ideograms by Leon Van Schaik explained

To imagine that Leon van Schaik's ideograms, used in the design practice research, represent a thinking process would be to miss the point. They are not representational, but rather they *are* the thinking – 'thinking in action', if you will, concretised in a drawing. To make this claim in our post-Socratic world is radical in that it suggests that the movement of the arm and hand are integral; it is to claim that the body thinks.

It is tempting to explain such an idea by describing van Schaik's frequent references to the work of Howard Gardner, who proposed that intelligence manifests itself in multiple ways including the corporeal. The use of referential logic to explain how these ideograms have come to be is, however, a method that – while it might bring confidence to historians – does little to persuade practitioners of creativity, such as van Schaik, who understand better the serendipitous and sometimes unlikely links between such things. Rather than being a source, Gardner's proposition simply articulates something already felt in this drawing practice.

It is van Schaik's purpose to find other ways to bring light to the mysteries of the creative process. This is what the ideograms do. They capture the idiosyncratic and unpredictable ways of design and are founded in an acute observation of that design practice as it happens, rather than through the citation of historical linkages made post-factum. The ideograms allow for the location of historical reference, precedents and even key texts (as observers will discover), but also allow for the spatial placement of these in relation to contrary interests – a sort of montage of things that constitute the moment of the thinking. Richard Hamilton's Pop-montage 'Just what is it that makes today's homes so different, so appealing?' has been influential in van Schaik's practice. There is a resonance with Hamilton's use of montage to arrange text, figures, objects and images inside a virtual 'world-in-a-room' as a way of simultaneously recording, questioning and propositioning.

Van Schaik's montages are accounts of his observations and conversations with the architects who are the subject of the drawing. They are, however, more than a simple recording in that van Schaik also draws things additional to the work observed. He teases out boundaries and gaps as a provocation to future work. Van Schaik locates himself within the ideogram as a collaborator rather than a commentator, a producer rather than recorder.

These are not easy ideograms to penetrate. They are like bodies to be discovered rather than symbols or texts in that there is no quick message and no particular beginning; one just picks a point and begins feeling around like a blind person reading a face. The form of the drawing takes shape only after several tracings across its surface. This is indeed what makes them so engaging. They arc an adventure, and their venturous[1] quality is reminiscent of the drawings of Archigram, whom van Schaik names among those who have influenced his practice.

There are a couple of way-finding tips that may be of use in coming to know these ideograms. Van Schaik uses the outline of a face to remind himself of the subjective reality of the ways we see – that we see through our own baggage. The outline of the face – and, in some ideograms, a pair of glasses – introduces the idea of the observer observing the observer doing the observing: a sort of cybernetic, iterative loop. An idealised theatre is used in some ideograms as a way of practising the thinking in a three-dimensional space, with the proscenium arch, stage curtain, backing screens and side screens providing props on which to locate key elements.

Van Schaik produces two kinds of ideogram: one is created as an act of private thinking, a sort of reflective practice; and the other as an act of public thinking, a communal activity. This second kind allows participants a special insight into how these ideograms come to be. To pay witness to their construction, to see the sequence of mark-making and arrangement, provides a kind of punctuation to the drawing. In the past, I have pointed out to van Schaik that his ideograms are more easily grasped if you see their construction as it happens. I have recommended that, rather than talking to already completed versions, a re-construction would be more engaging. He has been reluctant. In retrospect, my recommendation may be misplaced. While witnessing their formation is indeed a privileged moment, to reproduce them in a rehearsed way may rob them of their greatest attribute – that is, a spontaneous quality of action-thinking – which is something much more wonderful, and never fully recoverable in a repeat performance.

1   'Venturous' is a term borrowed from Terry Cutler's paper 'Venturous Australia' and is used here to refer to those practitioners who are adventurous enough to want to step beyond current practice boundaries - in other words, those practitioners whose work will change practice, the discipline and knowledge. The venturous are the researchers among us.

IN PRACTICE: CASE STUDIES

FORGOTTEN ZONES: A MATIÈRE FOR
AN ARCHITECTURE. COMPLETED: 1991

Allan Powell is Principal Director of Allan Powell Architects, a design-focused architecture and interior design practice based in Melbourne. The practice has been dedicated to the design and procurement of buildings in Australia and abroad since 1980, with work and experience across residential, institutional, cultural and commercial sectors. Powell has a distinctive yet considered approach to design that has been acknowledged through the receipt of awards, publication and industry recognition.

Until I began the design practice research Master's, I felt that all my interests – the things that seemed so profoundly important to me – didn't mean anything to anyone else. I mean, my buildings are pretty unawarded… Where do they fit in, you know? They're not imitating Zaha Hadid. What are they? Are they funny throwbacks to some era that's finished?

Melbourne in the 1980s: architects were ablaze with postmodernism and debate. Complexity (and contradiction) and the growing rise of architectural and cultural theory was a dominant source for architectural form. The tongue had to be as sharp as the pencil, and buildings brimming with reference and ideology. For architects such as Powell, who resisted the dominant paradigm and instead followed a much more *intuitive, experiential* practice, where things like light and shadow and the path of the sun mattered more than Venturi, the going could be tough. This is an architect who freely admits he likes buildings that look like buildings: *I've tried to make architecture more of a cultural artefact, but I can't see it that way. I see it as simply a formal device for making space. I like rectilinear forms that look like buildings and reference buildings.*

The work of Powell is, however, not so straightforward and this was recognised by a few people, including Leon van Schaik. Yes, there is a directness to his architecture – big stripped-back concrete walls, dark corridors and bluntly cut openings placed on-site according to Powell's deep understanding of how the sun moves, and what the best journey is across site from boundary to boundary – but underlying that is a poetic and subtle interest in the phenomenal, in the forgotten and the everyday, and in what he describes as *atavistic spatial experiences* where things are situated on the edge of recognition.

While some of these ideas are more acceptable and even fashionable now, they were not so then. Powell felt isolated and believed that his architectural pursuits and interests were not considered valid. He remembers, *I was in a cul-de-sac. My wholly intuitive approach was never fashionable*

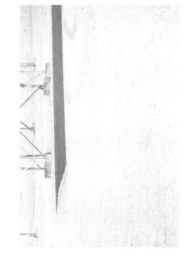

Figure 13: Images from Allan Powell's research catalogue

in the light of theory, especially the explosion of interest in theory at the time... His most complete and successful project from this period, just before commencing the research, was the Crigan House (1989).

> *It was a very self-conscious attempt to reference a building in the postmodern way: "Alright, then! I'll just put in what is important to me. I'll try and make a building out of it." So it was a giant staircase; it was a ship on the edge of the water; it's got a lot of references to St Kilda, corners, buildings and parts of buildings. I tried very hard to put spatial experiences that had meaning for me into that house...to try and quote them – but spatially or sensorially, and not in an intellectual way.*

He was content if the ideas he put together were not easily resolvable. *I knew they weren't able to be resolved. I knew that it was Arte Povera – things and ideas were crammed together and you just sort it out, you know?* Powell was angered by the dogged persistence of some architects to achieve the perfectly resolved object.

> *They'd be carrying on about crafting this and crafting that and resolving it, and I'd think, 'Resolve what? Just put that there and that there, because they're different states of mind; they don't go together.' I don't care if it's resolved. I'd rather have rude ideas knocked up against one another. You're not going to get resolution between these types of impulses.*

During this time, and through engaged conversations with several people including van Schaik, Powell was invited to join the Invitational design practice research program, ironically alongside architects such as Howard Raggatt.

The beginning of the research process was admittedly difficult for Powell: *I didn't know why I was doing what I was doing.* It was during a conversation with his supervisor van Schaik that the idea emerged to simply establish a body of data, a catalogue of photographs that Powell found affecting or moving and then to use them as the basis for reflection:

> *These conversations helped me see that I didn't have to resolve all these questions I had and that I should relax, gather the data, photograph what has meaning, and come to understand that I was interested in perception and metaphysical issues, and to understand that what I was trying to do had worth.*

This was a radical shift for Powell, who suddenly felt validated:

> *I started to make a catalogue of effects. I got confidence in metaphysical notions. I began to do things more as I really wanted to do, which was just planar walls and everything very uninventive-looking to the architectural mind. And then I*

started saying, "I don't care if I'm not an architect. Perhaps I'm not one. I'm a space-arranger. I'm not an architect because I'm not interested in what you're interested in. I don't care what the shape of anything is, as long as it's got the height."

This shift in perspective allowed Powell to review his past work more deeply:

I understood and began to see that the Crigan House was really an amalgam of this data that I'd collected. I could see that there were things that interested me everywhere and what I was interested in here was that the space had a very strong character, but at the end there's a chicken-wire fence and you look through it and there's a whole other world on the other side and you think, 'Where's the architecture?' It was to do with the metaphysical and perception and, up until I started the research, I had been struggling to make an architecture of it.

Powell felt, perhaps accurately, that *these ideas couldn't have been less fashionable at the time, so Leon was a god-send to me because he came from another world where he thought what I said had meaning; whereas Corrigan, who had highly developed political notions, ruled that a building was really a political diagram.*

Was there a particular turning-point for Powell during this process? *No! Because I was starting so far back. For me to even turn up and think I could walk in the door was a turning point, you know?* Powell's breakthrough was to realise with blinding clarity that it was perception, experience and states of mind that interested him and drove his architecture, revealed through the act of collecting and documenting a catalogue of phenomena. For example, a snapshot of a house in suburban Sydney depicted *an equally groomed scene.*

Everything – the lawns, path and wall – were equally manicured in such a way that it flattens out the conventional reading and the space. The way some retired man had painted every little bit and every blade of grass and the path became like a river. It took the conventionalised meaning out of it and turned it into an overall artefact. It was all so magnified and it was so powerful to me.

Another photograph of *a pretty horrifying block of cream brick flats in St Kilda,* described as being at the *peak of its unfashionability so you could conceptualise it easily,* had wrought-iron balconies stuck out over the car park that looked like a wall at the zoo with spaces where the animals come out and sit in the sun.

This configuration allowed for the most atavistic spatial reading...you didn't have to read it conventionally. It was just like a cliff-face with these spaces where you walked out. And then the danger below was the big concrete car park. You were sort of floating over the unacceptable, the un-occupiable, the untenable, in these little tiny cantilevered islands…

At the start, Powell photographed these scenes motivated simply by his fascination with the subject. Progressively, however, the house-shot and many others revealed a clear set of themes and ideas. With the flats, it was about phenomenalising the edge, whereas the house Powell photographed in a way *to break down its house-ness. The composition broke down that it was really a house. The fact of the path with those immaculately maintained blades of grass…to step off it was to step out of the Euphrates into Egypt.*

At that critical point, Powell reflected that the image was much like a Rachel Whiteread sculpture or a Bill Henson photograph, 'charged' with the potential of what it could be, *and I saw then I was trying to get at the idea of the phenomenalising of something.*

The research process clarified and validated Powell's architectural pursuits. His new confidence found remarkable expression in the De Stasio house, completed after his design practice research in 1995. An assemblage of rough abstracted walls and chambers set into the pastoral landscape of the Yarra Valley engage not only with the phenomenon of the landscape but also with rituals of inhabitation and architecture.

I used walls to define repetitive chambers that you suddenly saw were habitable. When does a wall suddenly become habitable? I was trying to abstract the conventionalised use of the kitchen, sitting room, everything, so that it looked interchangeable, so you shook free that level of informing the space and you were reduced to occupying the box - the architecture - more.

Powell sees the design practice research process as having had a huge and lasting impact on his career. He was *pulled out of a very deep hole by the project.*

It is now possible to look at these phenomena and understand what's interesting, what the principle is, and indeed apply it to my work. It's taken me till now to - almost with ease - have my eye caught by something and think, 'I see what is interesting there' that I may or may not use in a building. My work is not about some theoretical debate between someone in Japan and someone in Iceland and what they think, and then doing a political diagram of a building that's absolutely hideous but has a lot of worthy theory in it…I was very conflicted through that period and it took a long time…I'll be honest. It took years to percolate through and to understand the impacts of the process Leon had engaged me in.

Figure 13: Images from Allan Powell's research catalogue

Howard Raggatt is a director of ARM (Ashton Raggatt McDougall) with a reputation for innovation in design practice and theory. He has played a lead role in many of ARM's design awards, including the Victorian Architecture Medal for RMIT's Storey Hall, the Shrine of Remembrance, and the Melbourne Recital Centre and MTC Theatre. His most distinctive work includes the National Museum of Australia in Canberra. Currently he is Design Director of the Perth Waterfront development, the $350m multipurpose indoor stadium, Perth Arena, and the redevelopment of the Victorian Arts Centre.

If you can generate something through a type of strategy or operation, it seems to carry more... it's more durable than a gesture – something that's too personal. It's nice if you can hide the personal under a blanket of the operational.

One of the founding directors of ARM (1988) and the Half Time Club (1979), Howard Raggatt was among the first architects to participate in the Invitational design practice research program. This offer came at a critical time for Raggatt, marking the end of an intense period of teaching at RMIT that also coincided with ARM's receipt of large-scale commissions. The Kronborg Medical Clinic had been designed and would be completed in 1993 and that year they would also win the competition for the St Kilda Town Hall commission. As Raggatt recalls, *This research was crystallising from the practice point of view, but also incorporated the attitude of our teaching through that major era at RMIT in the 1980s – one of those strong times, and a pretty changing time.* He reflects that the ten solid years of teaching could well have vaporised had he not had the opportunity to undertake the research. Typically, teaching was not documented or otherwise captured in Australia at that time, and Raggatt, who was instrumental in the projects, attitudes and *fantastic efforts* of that decade at RMIT, emphasises that the Invitational Program was one way of (perhaps not so consciously then) giving evidence to that community of learning.

In the previous decade, a number of Melbourne architects had begun to exhibit and present ideas in *a somewhat reflective context, other than a purely architectural context.* These included Dale Jones-Evans and a series of exhibitions at Storey Hall, the first of which was initiated in 1984 by the *Biltmoderne-boys* (Roger Wood and Randal Marsh, who would go on to become Wood/Marsh). Another series of exhibitions took place in art galleries including ACCA, and at Monash, Melbourne and RMIT Universities. Architects including Raggatt benefited from these experiences, *because many architects were struggling to find some ground to actually do architecture.* For Raggatt, this research occurred at a particularly prolific time for his thinking and for ARM. The process of looking back across his body

Figure 14: Images from Howard Raggatt's research catalogue

of work involved reflections on the Kronborg Medical Clinic and the firm's inquiries into copy and translation.

Encouraged by Leon van Schaik to avoid stereotypical scholarly approaches, and instead to find a way of representing what actually went through his mind as he designed, Raggatt used stream-of-consciousness writing as a medium to test ideas concerning the status of the original, translations, ideas of authorship and architecture after modernism, and the condition of working as an architect in Australia. This decision to write was also motivated by his frustrations with the architectural writing of the time, which focused on the promotional rather than addressing architectural processes and ideas. For Raggatt, the relationship between ideas, aspirations and architecture revealed a certain *tragic* aspect of architecture – tragic because he saw many of the ideological aspirations: deeply problematic and interesting but largely unable to be fulfilled, mostly for *boring and pragmatic* reasons. These polemical essays, or *operations* as he calls them, were reflective of how architecture might be made.

> *I wanted to find the synergy between the operational – which is highly visual or design-focused, the way you make a design – and the discourse about it, which is not promotional or descriptive, but is actually equally problematic and includes the techniques. It's possible to give architecture a dimension other than its mannerisms and its styles – a very tiresome way to contemplate architecture, frankly.*

Emerging from this process, and following projects such as the *Not Villa Savoye House* and the *Not Vanna Venturi House*, were Raggatt's investigations into *the original and the copy*. These were also influenced by the *difficult* texts of Derrida, Deleuze and Foucault. However, he was reading the *translations* of those texts so, along with issues of authorship raised, it was the act of the translation and the reading of that which is not the original that interested Raggatt, and which he felt concerned Australian architecture.

Raggatt read not necessarily to become an expert on *what those guys were on about* but rather as an insight into the issues of the time. He observed that up until the mid-'70s the two dominant architectural portrayals of Australia were Peter Corrigan's vivid exploration of the Australian conditions and subcultures, and Glenn Murcutt's more *trite* and perhaps earnest vision. Rather than these *very affirmative visions*, Raggatt was increasingly concerned with what he describes as the *wider, more tragic condition* of being at the periphery where the main sources of art, architecture and literature are accessed through the imported copy.

> *Most of us are quite incompetent in terms of the originals. We've got this absurd pretence to an insight into real culture; yet our whole grounding and a lot of our reading, our intellectual content, is actually just a copy… and the new work, the real work, is the translation. I thought that theme was more interesting than the dichotomy emerging between*

Peter Corrigan's work and Murcutt's work, and instead looked at the whole issue of a 'cargo culture' dilemma. Inherent in that is a kind of tragedy. The social aspirations that we received through modernism are undermined by that realisation that everything we're doing is a derivative of a derivative of a derivative. There's somehow too much awareness of that process to entirely accept the emotional and the ideological power of modernism. And, by the time we'd come to it, most of that power had dissipated anyway, so [modernism] was only ever a kind of pursuit, a kind of fantastic commitment to architecture as a truly integrated social agenda that had dissipated… So our almost fanatical effort to create an operational architecture during this time was to avoid those otherwise ideological aspirations and to almost replace them with an equal passion, but one which implicitly knows it can't do it [make architecture] in that way anymore, that actually moves into a covert attitude to culture – and that architecture is tragic because one has to be subversive to do the work one wants to do, and not overt.

During this critical time just prior to Raggatt's involvement in the research, these tests of the copy begun with the *Not Vanna Venturi House* project were expanded and accelerated, and for him became an exegetic exercise. Venturi's plan for his mother's house, which he spent ten years designing, seemed *loaded with discourse*, and something in Raggatt's operations and his new translations made to that plan seemed to reveal that discourse and even other agendas not so obviously apparent.

That frigging-about with photocopiers and distortions brought out a whole other agenda, like expressionism for instance. Robert [Venturi] doesn't tell us that it's got expressionism in it, but does it have? Is he hiding something we don't know? Is this process of stretching and distorting and operating profound or not? Is it really an exegetical truth or not? I wrote to Robert about the tests. I went and saw him when we were over there in the '90s, and gave him a copy of this book [the design catalogue]. He really liked it and the correlation between Le Corbusier's Savoye and his house.

The investigation into operative methods for making architecture became increasingly refined during this next phase and has obviously continued as a dominant mode of ARM's practice. Also increasingly apparent, however, was that while the processes were *actual and direct* and the photocopy could be scanned, pixelated and – in the case of the Venturi plan – built, their *ideology or rationale remained secret and unspoken.*

On the one hand, there's a directness, wit and interest to it. It's processed: the kids could do it, anyone could do it. On the other hand, my thoughts about what I was doing could remain entirely secret, and I didn't need to therefore confess to what I really saw as a kind of tragic condition. I mean that in the strongest possible terms, that one is reduced to such processes. In order to create the possible and hopefully the new or the now, one is reduced to that… And when you see that little building, the Kronborg Clinic, it's made out of cream bricks, the cheapest bricks around. The building is tiny, simple as you could get, built in a crappy western suburb. And this is the aspiration of architecture in Australia. On the one hand, you've got some extreme aspiration and on the other you've got a few cream bricks. I think we afforded a few hundred glazed blacks and a few hundred glazed whites, and that was the extent of the architectural palette.

Following the presentation of these projects and the next period of work, Raggatt began pursuing the idea of the knot as another way to make sense of or to *acknowledge* the complexity of both the processes and outcomes, but also to give further expression to ideas of the tragic or what became known as *the negative.*

I got distracted by the complexity or the dilemmas of complexity that a knot represents - something that can't be untangled and is accepted for what it is - a tangle that isn't untangle-able… The photocopying and the blurring factor was so strong, and the exegetical pursuits got to the point where it was too difficult to extract the hidden - what I then saw as the incoherent. Was it possible to define those 'voices' of the incoherent, to find ways to eliminate doubt? Doubt was a major word at this time. It's a major word in my work, probably. Doubt-bracket-Tragic-comma-Death. Meaning of life!

For Raggatt, the knot acknowledged the degree of doubt in these *plan-catastrophes* that came out of the next series of projects, the *Not Vanna Venturi House Fast Plan* projects. Here, plans printed onto pieces of rubber were stretched, rotated and photocopied, *resulting in so much blurring and so many problematic shades…it wasn't possible to directly translate that and the process needed this other [the knot].* Raggatt recalls that the idea of the knot came from a review session attended by regular critic Ross Jenner, a New Zealand academic interested in the work of Gottfried Semper. Raggatt vividly remembers this period as opening up a *new vein, new ground,* which coincided with ARM's developing capacity and engagement with computer-generated methods.

At this point, the discussion of the tragic or the negative moved into different territory. The knot *was used to convey an aspiration with a negative in front of it. For example, an Australian would make a very negative comment meant to be taken as a positive - "You're* an old bastard!" – which really means, "You're a great friend of mine." The negative has subsequently been translated in many ways since: the knot, the subtractive, the cast, and the idea of packaging (the protective or the invisible), as seen most vividly in New Museum for Australia Canberra, The Marion Cultural Centre Adelaide, and the Melbourne Recital Centre.

One further reflection led to an acceptance of the complexity – the greyness – of the blur, which suggested the need to apply a testing method that would exactify the grey areas and give them precise tones and boundaries, and make them therefore buildable; pixelation was one of those techniques. This idea of making exact the blur was then explored in Storey Hall (1995). This next tranche of work, which included the Superman House and the Resurrection City, became what Raggatt defines as extreme translations of Robert Venturi's mother's house. This work gave rise to clarifications about the notions of translation and process. Is this what the new was? The new doesn't have to have anything original in it at all, other than – I'd be saying secretively – the tragic driving force for the new…

The final project in Raggatt's research, the Not Philip Johnson Glass House, revealed one more revision, one more test of these ideas. Here an entirely different operation was used that gave conceptual and built clarity to the investment in operative processes and these ideas of translation. At the time of this project, Raggatt was investigating anamorphic projections. A conical anamorphic of Johnson's Glass House was made; and, within that process, a cone was placed in the ablution block that unexpectedly turned the building inside-out like a pair of socks!

So again, here was something in which there was seemingly no creativity other than what could be seen as process. The only creativity – obviously I hate that word 'creativity' – the only factor was this amazing outcome, arrived at by turning something inside-out. We made a little ashtray out of it and put it back in the architect's house with the realisation that the best thing to do with new architecture is to make an ashtray out of it!

This project represents Raggatt's interest in the capacity of operations to contain some subversive secret interpretation. An operation that turns something upside-down, inside-out, to me – from the perspective of an Australian architect – has quite a lot of meaning.

For Raggatt, one of the major impacts of the research had been the serious contribution that the work has made to building a milieu that defined certain aspects of what he describes as the attitudinal ground of the time. Through their work with ARM and their teaching and involvement in the design practice research program, Raggatt and his colleague Ian McDougall have attempted to engender a milieu of architectural practice, rather than the genius individual. We've tried to think of the practice also as being a generative milieu, and this kind of document tries to define the language and domain, or interests, of that aspiration.

Additionally, the series of *dilemmas and questions* that emerged from the research has also defined a modus operandi for the practice. Rather than the work being about a kind of mechanical aping of a particular style or manner,

> We want to maximise the potential of any particular project. In other words, you can either couch your thinking in an increasing certainty or know-how, or you can couch your thoughts in dilemmas, problematics and uncertainties. And if you take that latter path, which I like to think is our path, then you bring to the project this set of dilemmas.

And where have the negative and the empty ended up now? Perhaps they can be seen in the *fantastic possibility* of what Raggatt sees as architecture's best purpose:

> ...to define the invisible or to define the aspiration whilst being nothing but packaging itself, nothing but a throwaway product. I suspect both the title of this research and the negations that run through it are trying to convey an aspiration; they just happen to define it through negative terminology. You look back and you think architecture appeared to have a kind of legibility in terms of a cultural community that I don't think it has now. I'm interested in architecture as a pathetic vehicle of some sort of condensing of the human condition – usually in a sort of tragic mode, but it doesn't have to be that...

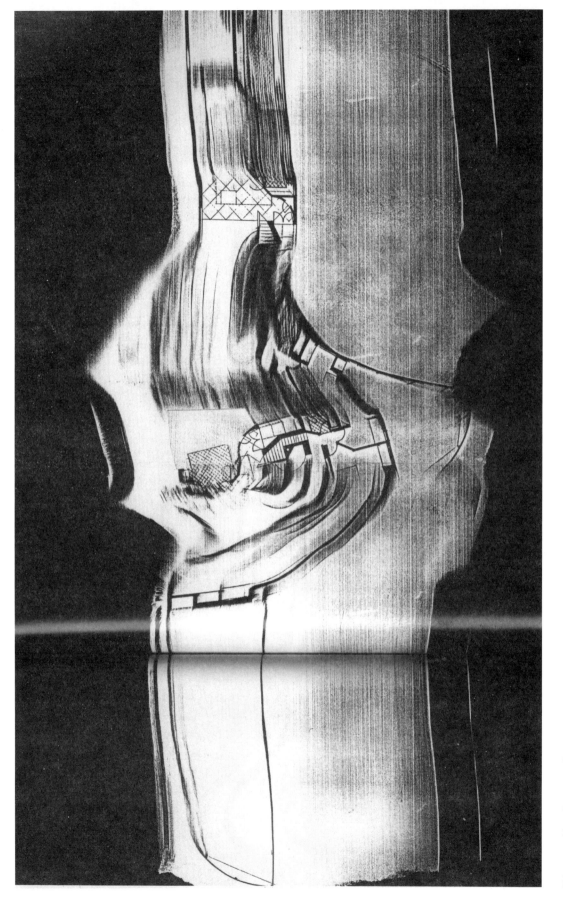

Figure 14: Images from Howard Raggatt's research catalogue

TOWARDS A BRAND NEW CITY
COMPLETED: 1993

Carey Lyon co-founded Lyons Architecture in 1996 and provides design leadership across a range of TAFE, higher education, research, commercial and other major projects. He is one of Australia's acknowledged leaders in urban design, in sustainability and in the design of research and learning environments. In 2006/2007 he was elected National President of the Australian Institute of Architects and was awarded the Presidential Medal from the American Institute of Architects.

We are interested in ideas that connect architecture to the wider world and, even though that wasn't explicit in my research, it was there, and we're now more confident or more skilled at doing it. We have a very strong ideology that architecture's not about the narrowness of the discipline. It's got to be engaging with the wider world of ideas and they can come from different sources for different projects. Even designing through metaphor – we use that all the time as a way of saying, "Well, architecture's like something else in the world so therefore let's make a project which is making that connection."

Invited into the second cohort of the design practice research program, Carey Lyon completed in 1993 along with Ian McDougall, Shane Murray, Rob McBride, Eli Giannini and Antonia Bruns. This group, propelled by the momentum of the first cohort that included Howard Raggatt and Norman Day, was heavily engaged in the didactic architecture culture of the early 1990s, and was particularly concerned with issues of the contemporary city. At that time Lyons was associate director of Perrott Lyon Mathieson, so projects such as the Telstra Headquarters Building and the Moorabbin Industry Training Centre were included in his research.

He also taught design studio at RMIT with Michael Markham and Nigel Westbrook, and then in the Invitational design practice program with Howard Raggatt and Ian McDougall. These early studios, which investigated massive 100,000-square-metre office buildings and shopping centres, were *slightly heretical – definitely not as mainstream as they became.* Thus, both his practice and teaching focused on commercial and public typologies within the city. Lyon recalls that the invitation to participate in research was *a chance to look into the projects to find something and then, having found it, to see if that can be contextualised within a body of ideas.*

Figure 15: Images from Carey Lyon's research catalogue

Lyon's Telstra Headquarters Building on Lonsdale Street, begun just prior to his involvement in the research, was a huge corporate building sited adjacent to 19th-century remnants that became an ideal testing ground for design practice research. The challenge of the project lay in the complexity of a big corporate object set against the grain of the streetscape with the demand to program *its empty 80,000 square metres into something that would work in the city. Lyon recalls, I knew what I was doing and why I was interested, but I certainly hadn't had a chance to contextualise it in a meaningful way, and that was very good for me. The challenge was to look at an architecture that was more speculative, to look at architecture which was testing ideas about the city specifically and intellectually.*

Paradoxically, while many dismissed the reality of working on large commercial buildings and the type of things he was learning as *the dirty commercial paradigms you have to deal with, Lyons himself found them interesting as a place of speculation...I was working on office buildings for developers, but working with curtain*

walls and the idea of the flexible office building that was just
like a container with a skin was very interesting.

Following the recession in the 1980s and the subsequent intense local debate about public buildings and the institution – particularly in light of the money and scale invested in commercial buildings throughout this decade – Lyon started working on public buildings. As he remembers,

When we started working with public buildings, the rhetoric of
the public institutions was: "We want flexible space because
we want to change and adapt. We don't know what the public
institution might be in five years' time, so don't put us in a
straitjacket." So we got interested in the idea, within the
practice and in the research process, of taking some of those
paradigms of capitalism and folding them into public buildings.

Lyon, as with several candidates from this period, used a type of didactic writing as part of the research process. One particular piece, *An-Other City For a Thin World (1993)*, published in Transition, issue 40, was a *crazy type of architectural poem, almost like a ranty word play…you put the words down and then somehow the words gave you a direction to go in. This work was one of those eureka moments.*

Committing to an idea through writing gives the idea a
world of its own. [My writing] was reinforcing the idea that
architecture's an artifice. It's a fiction. Architecture is
like writing fiction. It's not like writing non-fiction or a
documentary. It's more like doing something more filmic. You can
either be in the realist documentary mode or you can go into
some wider imaginary fictional world. That was one thing that I
consolidated in the research.

Another objective was to use text to investigate the contemporary city through the lens of *all the big paradigm shifts of the post-industrial city and culture – media, late capitalism and the consumer society, and then the global village and information technology. How do you look at those things and not think that architecture must be different in that context?*
One direct translation of these ideas into Lyon's current practice is the way each building can be seen as a public building: specifically, *My brother's just done this house, a little art museum house that's like a public building;* and, more generally, *We emphasise the public building when we do a commercial building.*
The idea of *the architectural skin* was a further issue that was clarified within the research. Despite Lyon's lamenting that, *As a practice, we get a bit tired of being saddled with the 'skin' headline,* during the research process the term became a convenient way to describe an urban condition as opposed to an architectural strategy.

Figure 15: Images from Carey Lyon's research catalogue

There was this interesting contemporary condition in the 19th century, where ... the institution was stable. A town hall was a town hall; a church was a church. Then, during the '90s, the public institution was commercialised. It had to be more contemporary and flexible, but at the same time maintain that architectural obligation to deal with the city; and these two ideas are kind of disjunct. Therefore the skin - its inside/outside - is important to that. It's more about the intriguing ambiguity in this thin condition of the body of the institution and how it represents itself into the city.

In addition to the published material resulting from the research, there were other immediate consequences for Lyon. He now had *a sense of the kind of ideas that were better pursued in another practice than the practice I was in,* and so he left Perrott Lyon Mathieson to set up practice with his brothers Corbett and Cameron Lyon in 1996. Lyon makes it clear that *collaboration* and the culture of a discursive practice has always been important to him and that the ideas pursued in his research, and now in practice, have come from engagement with collaborators, mentors and colleagues along the way. He describes how the Lyons office operates:

> *There are four other directors: Corbett worked with Venturi and he's got a whole lot of ideas, and then Neil [Appleton] and Adrian [Stanic] came through the RMIT urban architecture research program and were taught by Ian McDougall and Howard Raggatt and have a whole set of fantastic ideas as well, and now we put them all into the practice in a more integrated way. We're a very discursive practice. We talk about architecture and what we're doing all the time in the design process, and while we're doing it we're pinning up and critiquing each other and throwing more ideas at every project.*

For Lyon, design practice research served to strengthen the role of discursive *reflective* practice in the office. Lyon reflects:

> *The process was like subjecting yourself to enforced analysis. You can easily get caught up in practice and just doing it and doing it and doing it, but to take time out – not that it was time out, it was on-top-of – to do the reflective work definitely works as a process.*

Importantly, it also consolidated his commitment to *the idea of ideas, of building ideas, not just designing buildings.*

Figure 15: Images from Carey Lyon's research catalogue

Ian McDougall has been a Director of ARM (Ashton Raggatt McDougall) since its inception in 1988. He was Project Director of the master planning of Melbourne Docklands from 1996 for the Melbourne Docklands Authority and of the master planning of Yarra Edge, Victoria Harbour. He was Director in Charge of the Shrine of Remembrance and of the Melbourne Recital Centre/MTC Theatre and is currently Director in Charge of the Southbank Cultural Precinct Redevelopment. He is Professor of Architecture and Urban Design at the University of Adelaide.

Ian McDougall, director of ARM along with Howard Raggatt and Steve Ashton, was invited to join the first cohort of the Invitational design practice research program in 1990. Like Raggatt, his teaching and practice collaborator, this invitation came at the end of a significant decade. By then McDougall had been with ARM for just over four years, and the firm had begun to secure larger-scale commissions and to become publicly recognised. They had just received the RAIA Commendation for Commercial Architecture for the Kronborg Medical Clinic, but McDougall recalls that they were still working through the dynamics and personalities of all three directors. This period also marked what he saw as a confusion with Australian architecture and *the real issues concerning the profession beyond the populist partisanship arguments of Australian architecture and identity. McDougall accepted the invitation to undertake design practice research,*

> *...[because of the] sheer pragmatism and brilliance of Leon's [van Schaik] idea to have practitioners come in, complete a design practice research Master's and, in one fell swoop, contemplate and document their work and get a credential to teach within the academy in a proper institutional way. It was a beautiful thing. The space provided to think about your own work was not so conscious at the time; however, once I started, it became apparent that it was a rare and valuable opportunity.*

Given McDougall's particular concerns with representation and architecture, this period of research and reflection, occurring at the end of *neo-classical postmodernism* and during the revival of theories of architectural ornament, was particularly interesting. It was also confronting, because after a time of intense design practice, the research process felt like *a sort of vacuum, a space to sit down, study and think about an issue, and then research it. And if you're all over the place thinking about forty different things at once - as I was - it*

was quite a difficult thing to do. The structure of the design practice research degree established by van Schaik worked very well for McDougall. What began as an inquiry into hybrids, hybridisation and the search for the *original* became an investigation into the copy, ideas of recall, memory and the impact of contemporary image overload. As he remembers,

> *My thinking about hybridisation led to a complete dead-end.*
> *I kept coming back to this realisation that there's no origin*
> *for the hybrid. The creative craft is not about hybridisation.*
> *Hybridisation is constantly limited by having to acknowledge*
> *the power of the origin. I got really confused and then decided*
> *the hybrid was in fact the new...*

McDougall recalls that the early 1990s was marked by the widespread explosion of imagery, in particular data imagery.

> *I started to think about what that mass of imagery meant, what*
> *the impact of that imagery was. Here, Howard and I merged our*
> *interests in the idea of copy and, for me, the copy's fabulous*
> *frailty to authority! I was interested in the Auckland School*
> *of Fine Arts, colonial history...and that beautiful trait of the*
> *creative spirit constantly requiring authentication and then*
> *making the authentication through similarities to an origin. I*
> *can't get it into a theoretical position, but I always found it so*
> *beautiful.*

This issue of hybridisation was pivotal not only because of the theoretical dilemmas it raised, but also because its *irresolvability*, which led him to drop the subject completely and direct his work specifically into representation and the work on souvenirs. McDougall realised that his interest in hybridisation had been more of an inquiry into *personal validation of the place of one's own work in history and its relationship to the wider culture*. While Raggatt was pursuing operations on the copy as a way to connect or explore those histories and also to create the new, McDougall adopted a strategy that would engage his interest in pop art.

Raggatt concluded his research with a catalogue of new procedures for designing. McDougall reversed this strategy by transforming his work into an object – a souvenir – that could fit back into the pop art culture and quite literally be placed on the coffee table as a kind of subversive *objet d'art*. With the Rocker House, the architecture was remade, rescaled and drawn, somewhat denuded, stripped of unnecessary ornament, and finally returned to the domestic interior. For McDougall, the act of reconfiguring and abstracting the original and reducing the detail was instantly attractive: *The process of drawing them again so they could be made by pattern makers and deciding what was left out pushed me up against the problem of representation.*

McDougall found that this subversion of architecture's authority – another interest shared with Raggatt – aligned with postmodern theories of ownership and entitlement.

> *You can capture and therefore take a section of the world just by the mere fact of taking the souvenir or taking the photograph; or, like colonial artists commissioned to paint the prospect, there is a certain kind of capture - "I own and I secure it by its being painted." So that seemed to represent aspects of my work. The Brunswick Health Centre is really - and I didn't know this until I sat down and thought about it - capturing bits of that suburb and just sticking it together, but rubbing out bits along the way…so the project subverts its own imagery and is not too real.*

As with Raggatt, McDougall's research, teaching and practice have always been accompanied by a strong impulse to contribute to and to generate an architectural culture – a community of learning. McDougall sees van Schaik as instrumental in the development of Melbourne's culture, and the instigation of this Invitational design practice research was a critical move. This nurturing of a culture is something McDougall sees is as *people dedicating their lives to it. Our teaching at RMIT and now mine at Adelaide University is very much couched in the idea of trying to make a diverse culture…to energise students and encourage them, not just make them acolytes.*

The impact of the design practice research on McDougall has been significant and far-reaching. He notes that because certain ideas and strategies were *crystallised at that particular time and under those conditions, they haven't gone away.* Further, *you actually adopt a condition of reflection about your work,* which adds depth to both his teaching and his architectural practice. McDougall shares Raggatt's interest in the dilemmas raised by the material and the development of strategies to explore them.

> *I think the anchor or the rock are the issues we keep returning to, and finding when they become a problem in a studio or in practice… From my point of view – and maybe from Howard's, too – I think it was more about confronting issues you hadn't resolved or faced that you found yourself constantly coming back to. The [Invitational process] gave a framework for them to sit in your mind without being avoided or lost, while you could consider them or work through them. It wasn't so much about drilling down to the source; it was more like not drilling down to the source, but drilling down to the bit around the source, which is where it manifests itself, in these confrontations and the things that you didn't want to work through – and I realised: actually, that is what I'm constantly working on so I should try and confront that issue.'*

The Marion Cultural Centre (2002) was the first major work completed after McDougall finished his design research. As McDougall recalls, *it was a much clearer project in the way that it dealt with representation and local topologies, roadside shopping strips, suburban space, and the whole suburban context.* Rather than being an abstraction of suburbia or a pastiche,

it's actually about thinking through the recollections of those elements that are then turned into the building. The car-park is absolutely to do with that recall of suburban car-parks. And then the interior space, that fluidity of the space, is also that old hall space rattling around. I like the way it dealt with representation – it's explicitly representational, but it's also completely abstract. When you look up close, it's not what it appears to be.

The almost overt sensuousness and luscious formal experimentation of Marion, as well as its contextual engagement, give the building a particular clarity of intent and resolution. This building seems also to express an uncontainable delight or joy. McDougall says,

> *Well, you can't kill joy. There's a hell of a lot of optimism… resurrection; there's a lot of hope in the work. Howard comes at it from one particular point-of-view, and I come at it from another – a sort of tragedy that's embodied in humour, at the same time as having humility and hope within it.*

CUT THREADS AND FRAYED ENDS:
THE CHARACTER OF ENCLOSURE
COMPLETED: 2001

John Wardle established the award-winning John Wardle Architects in Melbourne in 1986. He has an international reputation as a design architect and has developed a design process that builds upon ideas that evolve from a site's topography, landscape, history and context and a client's particular aspirations and values. The result is an architecture closely tailored to its place and highly experiential in nature. He has been a visiting lecturer at Columbia University, New York, and he lectures periodically at various universities across Australia.

For me this research was about confidence, about deeply personal things... It provided an important understanding that there is logic to what is otherwise my very intuitive process. It invited me to examine that and to feel strongly about it, and to improve my descriptive processes about the methodologies we employ. It gave me greater confidence in finding that what we do is actually really valid. I think a lot of good architects are uncertain and I'm certainly one of them. As confidently as I might say or state something, I'm driven in many ways by levels of uncertainty...

The invitation to participate in the Invitational design practice research program at RMIT in 1999 coincided with the evolution of John Wardle Architects from a practice that had undertaken mostly smaller-scale residential work for 15 years to one engaged with large-scale, high-budget institutional and civic projects. Wardle had completed a series of highly resolved and expressive projects including the Balnarring Beach House (1994–97), the Portsea Beach House (1997–99) and then, towards the end of that period, the RMIT Printing Technologies building (1998–2000) and the RMIT Biosciences building (2002). As Wardle says, *We were on the cusp of engagement with drastically bigger work. We'd just got our first really big commission: the QV project.*

The research, which spanned this period when the firm was working on buildings in the city including QV and Urban Workshop, came at an ideal time. The dramatic scale-shift required the firm to halt proceedings and to reflect on *the scale you operate with, the scale of the practice, and how you can translate the scale of small project experience to a larger format.* Out of necessity, issues of the building and its role within the city became part of the office conversation, as did the process of analysis involved in Wardle's research.

Wardle admits his firm has always been a busy practice, slightly under-resourced for the amount of work they have on. This has facilitated his natural

Figure 17: Photograph from John Wardle's completion exhibition

modus operandi of producing *on the run, in intense conversation, and through intense processes*. John Wardle Architects has never operated on a two-year or five-year plan.

> *I've never been a person that stops, draws breath and analyses our situation. It's just not in my set of parts…The research enforced a need to address our methodologies, processes and the things we felt were valuable, that we had to re-focus on. It was an enforced discipline and a process that doesn't come naturally… I had to stop and consider and analyse. If left to my own devices, I don't. I'm the ultimate creative opportunist and onto the next thing.*

While his work was praised by external critics such as American academic Kevin Alter (Center for American Architecture, University of Texas, Austin) in the very first Research Symposium, the reality of having to slow down and present the work within the Research Symposium framework was difficult. This abrupt deceleration revealed the speed at which they had been working and led to a period of uncomfortable close critique. Wardle recalls:

> *It took me back to my student experience. I remember a session presenting to Sand Helsel, Leon van Schaik and outside panellists including Ranulph Glanville, and trying to convince them, show my examination of my work in a cohesive manner…I remember them saying: "Gee, you're not really making that point at all well; I'm not really seeing anything that's particular. I don't think you're applying a certain logic that can be identified or argued with well enough here." In the early phases of the program, there were areas of real criticism and a real difficulty in providing the threads and the connection between things.*

At that stage, Wardle began drawing a diagram that evolved throughout the research, which *graphically provided thematic linkage between programs. In some ways I felt I'd solved the problem early by looking at a graphic arrangement of the lineage of programs and ideas across the work.* For Wardle, a prolific drawer, working through diagram as a way to unravel his practice proved successful, and as with many undertaking this process, he found stronger threads between projects than he had imagined. His diagram addressed what he called the *techniques of practice and then the techniques of design.* One important strategy was revealed in a category he called *Stretching Design Time.* This described the constant iterative processes of designing and finding opportunities beyond the conventional architectural stages, through the documentation stages and even onto the building site. *Stretching Design Time* is also a necessary condition in order to hone the details.

We're still looking at creative opportunities late in the process…if you take a project like the Melbourne Grammar School, it's only as successful as the really complex steel and glass façade with its embedded ceramic pattern in the glass, or the really evocative brick pattern. These details can never be worked out conceptually in one go at the front end of the process, and our work is so intensely resolved in the application of detail that you can only do that slowly and across many stages of operation.

By contrast, the *Techniques of Design*, a different category identified in the research, was a way for Wardle to understand and to document the design thematics of the buildings. Techniques included operability, open-endedness, mannered cuts, diffuse edges and frayed ends, all of which variously describe qualities of planning, ideas for resolving the *end condition* of buildings, and the way elements, axes and compositions terminate. It was only in the final preparations for the completion seminar, however, that Wardle experienced a deeper level of clarity and insight into his work even as doubt set in:

With nine days to go, I got very nervous and thought, 'Gee, I don't think this is interesting to other people, and how am I going to present this?' I was going to do these big panels along the wall that would describe the ideas that had been set over the last few years. I read everything I'd written and I had a real moment of doubt. And then I thought, 'We have a great build-rate as a practice, and I need some kind of physical reality to end with.' At the end of it I needed a building, something that I could demonstrate with, something physical before me to sign off the process.

At the end of each building project, Wardle had developed a ritual of giving a piece of furniture designed by the office to his clients, a gift that summarised the design intentions, brought the project to a conclusion and marked the end of the creative exchange with the client. He decided to complete his design practice research in the same way. It was this final object – an elaborate and operable music stand for Wardle's middle child – that gave closure to Wardle's research, while physically demonstrating his design process and its themes. Having this object designed and built with only nine days to go was frantic, but no more so than Wardle's usual manic dash to meet the deadline. As always, the final intense negotiation between contractors, staff members and Wardle led to a creative fast-paced design *process of drawing, over-drawing and re-drawing* followed by production. Wardle admits this process always involves a lot of persuasion,

This is what I tend to do. I coerce people into doing something remarkable, to build something remarkable, whether it's a bricklayer on-site or a joiner or tiler…

The completion seminar took place after Wardle and six joiners worked through the night to complete this final piece.

They were still erecting it in front of the gathering academics. It looked like performance art. We actually constructed this object in front of the audience. It wasn't pretence; it was just the deadline being met. And I talked to that piece of joinery and literally unfolded the ideas through the unit.

This research captured the state of Wardle's practice at a very pivotal moment in time.

Without romanticising it, there was a real level of discovery into how I operate... This project stopped me and made me really think how I describe how I work. Until the invitation I just started work in the morning and then finished up exhausted at the end of the day having worked furiously hard. But to construct a description of my processes was something I had never really had to do. And because we hadn't engaged with a lot of big clients at that stage, I didn't really even have to describe it to clients. We just delivered on promises.

Now that the firm is involved in larger projects, this research has greatly assisted Wardle to discuss the design work and the processes with clients; and, on a personal note, the research has allowed John Wardle the individual to get out from under John Wardle Architects, the firm:

When you invent an architectural practice, as I did, and it gains momentum, you can lose a sense of self. Although it made me acutely aware of the contribution of others, it also revealed the loss that you have when you immerse yourself in practice. In that series of collaborative experiences, there's a bit of losing the sense of self: How do I operate? What do I think? What drives me personally? What are my own successes, not those of John Wardle Architects, but those of John Wardle? I could have blithely gone through life not having had that moment of reckoning.

Jennifer (Jenny) Lowe trained as an architect and has used various forms of art practice, including performance, painting and installation, as research and inter-disciplinary collaboration for her architectural design. Lowe has combined teaching, research and practice to promote an understanding of the earth and its unfolding dynamics as the *site* of a recent human inhabitation that might work with respectful, creative co-existence. More recently, her practice has focused critically on earth-human relationships within the current dynamics of global warming.

I still find this notion of reflective practice really interesting – the idea that one is actually going into the past to try and find these potentialities that haven't been actualised. Even to start reading, looking within the creative work for something that you're not sure what it is... Perhaps you don't necessarily find it at all; maybe what you find is its direction, which is its future.

Jenny Lowe, architect, artist and academic, moved to the UK in 1971 to complete the final two years of her undergraduate architectural course at the Architectural Association (AA) in London, where later she would also meet Leon van Schaik and Sand Helsel. Upon graduation, Lowe stayed on to teach during a *didactic period* at the AA. After five years, she went into architectural practice before finally returning to teaching at Brighton University and to her own practice of painting and architecture. In 1996, she was invited to undertake the Invitational design practice research program at RMIT. Upon completion, she enrolled in a design practice research PhD in 1998 seeking to expand upon things discovered during the earlier research. Lowe recalls that, in the late '90s, research through design was unusual and viewed with a certain degree of suspicion in both London and Australia:

Leon was very much putting his neck out in terms of arguing that research could be undertaken through design. Even now in England, there still aren't any very good examples of it. If students try and do it, design is really just tacked on, with students having to produce the formatted thesis, with a portfolio that goes with it, so it becomes just an appendage. It was particularly interesting what he was trying to do – uncompromisingly saying that research could be undertaken through design itself, where new knowledge is produced through that process of reflection and design.

Lowe's Master's, titled 'Landscape? Forming and Informing of Architectural Space', published in *interstitial modernism*, RMIT (2000), was undertaken in the third round of the Invitational program. She remembers directly following instructions to *take previous work, review it, and from that try to articulate what makes that work particular, or what its driving interests or driving forces are, and then to undertake a piece of speculative design to test that*. Lowe was invited on the basis of a significant body of work, and found that her selection of projects to explore, including the Ruins of the Future (1996), The Motels Projects, and the Federation Square competition work, had a very profound effect on the research outcomes. These works, with their processes emerging (then unconsciously) from her own creative practice of painting, as well as from her new theoretical interests in landscape, spatial poetics and post-structuralist discourse, have a delicious *thick* textural quality and a precise drawn resolution that reveals her education at the AA and the emergent deconstructive paradigm.

Lowe's research began with the ambition to explain relations between *subject and object* as they worked across her architectural space. Following comments made during her first completion seminar, the PhD research began with the question: *What makes space architectural?* And then specifically: *What is the particular nature of my architectural spaces?*

Lowe began by looking closely at her painting process and then the relationship between her paintings and architectural projects. Framed as *dialogues*, these paintings helped to refine the research into what she then called *the Space Between* – a place of creativity and reflection that uncovered a common thread:

> *These works were really important. I wasn't drawing something I already knew. I would always do it with materials that worked in a similar way to what I was thinking, so that the outcome always gave me something that I didn't have before...I started realising that what I was finding in them, coming from a completely different angle, was the same kinds of space that I was also exploring in architectural projects.*

In the next phase of research, she made explicit the desire to *forge a more seamless relationship* between her painting and the design of architectural spaces. What began as a design study to explore the *Space Between* as a type of architectural space revealed to her that the *Space Between* was actually a strategic device or approach for the design of her architectural spaces and spatial relationships. Marking the point at which this alignment between her painting and architectural intentions began, Lowe participated in an exhibition in Brighton, England, exhibiting both her *Space Between* paintings and her Federation Square completion stage-one and -two entries. It was also at the time when van Schaik introduced the idea of Ephemeral Architecture, an idea for which Lowe had a particular affinity as a result of an increasing awareness of themes of time, duration and memory in her work.

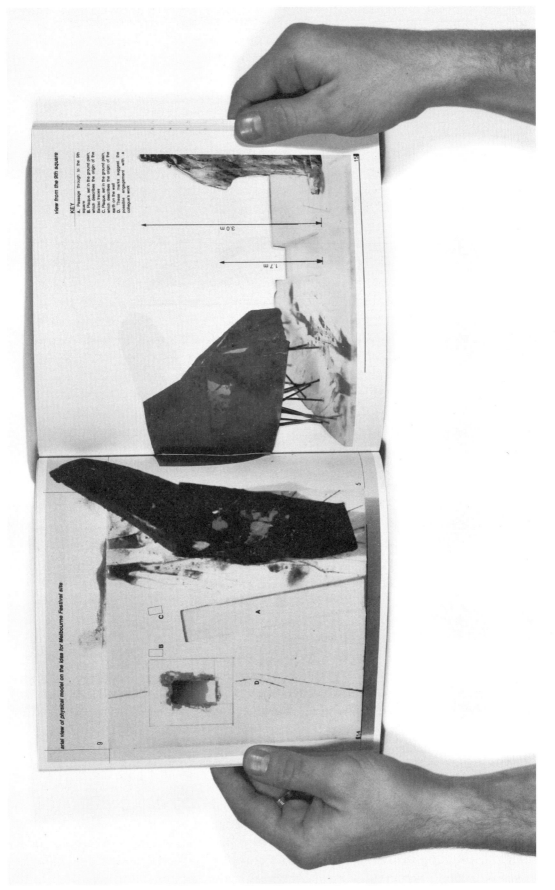

Figure 18: Image from Jenny Lowe's research catalogue

Lowe spent considerable time reflecting on how work should be discussed within these research frameworks. Having worked in commercial practice and having had work published, Lowe was acutely aware of the differences between the way design was talked about and the actual design process:

The way one talked about the work within the context of where one was doing it was completely different to the secret life of its aspirations and its evolution. Occasionally one would give some sort of access to that, but one was always very careful about whether it was going to jeopardise the way the work was looked at. So what I was really wanting to do here was to reveal the secret story of the projects and what was really being invested in them.

Lowe discovered that this secret story was an essential part of her reflective practice. She found that the very act of looking back to find something to take forward was not only compelling but was an essential part of what she was doing, although a *very difficult thing to do*. Lowe's practice, with its focus on experiential phenomena, spatial conditions and the various 'land' conditions that were *really pure sensation*, made articulating and drawing out the driving forces very challenging. In some instances, setting up the brief for the next project proved a very useful way to focus her language and strategy.

Another part of this search for language revealed – first in her Ruins of the Future project – that she was conceptualising different ideas of the other. This trajectory brought her to the work of Elizabeth Grosz, Henri Bergson and Gilles Deleuze and to ideas of the virtual. While this had first became apparent in her Master's, the idea was developed more completely in her PhD where she used diagramming and design to get at these ideas. *I went back and tried to diagram how those relations, and then this notion of the space of dialogue, became important as a particular relation of the other.*

Lowe became very preoccupied with ideas of the virtual: the virtual of the future, and *that funny Bergson statement, that the virtual as a future is already in the past.* This idea resonated with her struggle with reflective practice; she identified that she was looking for a potential in her past work that had not yet been used in the present and would be actual in the future. Was this the virtual? Involved in this was an unexpected kind of spatial reorientation. Lowe says, *In this process of following it, trying to find it, you're looking backwards, and coming towards you, but at the point where you can see its direction, you're actually then behind it, moving it or going forward with it.*

Much of this work was done while living in London, so Lowe was working remotely on Melbourne sites. This separation – alienation – revealed significant things for her about memory and place, about what is remembered and how that affects design outcome. Towards the end of this period a breakthrough emerged, firstly in her two proposals for the 2001 Melbourne Arts Festival, and then the built resolution in her concluding work exhibited as part of the 2002 Melbourne Arts Festival Site Project. She became increasingly aware of a recurring figure, which became known as REP: Red Earth Plain. Lowe identified its first appearance in the Ruins of the Future (Adelaide, 1996) competition as a very site-specific intervention, literally red earth laminated between two sheets of glass that operated as a critique of the *smoothing over or denial* of the land by colonialists. This figure, abstract and large in scale, was also a recollection of early childhood experiences of the Western District and the enormity of the Australian landscape. Later, in the series of festival projects beginning in 2001, these REP studies involved 1:1 experiments as Lowe tested the adherence of the red earth to glass, which would erode with time and with rain, leaving a red *trace* on the ground but also revealing the ground behind and the thinness of the earth's surface cover. The final and most potent manifestation of the REP was its realisation in the 2002 Melbourne Arts Festival. Here it was *displaced* and installed in Bowen Lane, RMIT, where it could receive the rain and late afternoon light, with the intention of evoking the durational nature of space.

These last series of projects brought together her themes of time (duration), of the other and of landscape, and particularly, her growing interest in the way that land (or *earth*, as it became known) is objectively portrayed within science and geography as opposed to more phenomenally engaging with ideas of memory, time and subjectivity. Finishing the PhD, Lowe feels clearer about these issues and she recognises that *installation was definitely very strong* in terms of representing these ephemeral ideas.

> *This sense of the long time and of the earth itself, especially as a young child, can be quite overwhelming and can make you feel very insignificant. A lot of this started to make sense after I'd completed...It was again having some distance from it, and being able to reflect on it, that these very valuable things became clearer again.*

ANTI-MEMORIALS: RE-THINKING
THE LANDSCAPE OF MEMORY
COMPLETED: 2005

SueAnne Ware is Professor and
Head of School at the School
of Architecture and Built
Environment, University of
Newcastle. She is a Fellow in the
Australian Institute of Landscape
Architects. Her exhibited
work, awarded built projects,
curatorships and publications have
contributed to a growing discourse
in landscape architecture, design
activism and design research.

*I wanted to know if what I thought I was doing, and what I was
saying or writing about what I was doing, were the same things.
Part of my PhD was to test the ideas versus the real outcomes,
and part of it was an ambition to make projects in the world that
would make a difference socially, which could become a catalyst
for change.*

Landscape architect and academic SueAnne Ware enrolled in the
Invitational design practice research program in 2000 and completed within
five years. A career academic, she has nonetheless continued to practice.
American-born Ware completed a Master's at Berkeley and then moved to
Australia to begin her full-time role within the RMIT landscape architecture
program in 1997. By this point, she already had 10 years' practice experience,
including seven years with other firms and two years working on her own
projects. Having grown up in Jordan Downs public housing in south-central
Los Angeles, she bore witness to cultural marginalisation and the devastating
social consequences of drug-use and addiction. Not surprisingly, Ware's
research, begun in her undergraduate thesis and continued in her postgraduate
research, has always asserted a definite ethical and community agenda. At
Berkeley, *a very good school and incredibly socially aware*, she
attempted to combine these social investigations with her design practice.
However, despite Berkeley's strong focus on social science pedagogy, there
was no precedent for such a multidisciplinary approach: *It was hard to
be a designer at Berkeley. Most people wanted you to become a
facilitator. I knew all of those social mapping practices and
techniques but I couldn't do anything with them.*

For Ware, whose work *challenged the conventional norms in
landscape architecture*, the PhD was a timely way for her to examine
her practice to date. It was also a way to build up design work inclusive of
social engagement whilst establishing an intellectual engagement with her new
home and the local landscape architecture discourse. Working on memorials

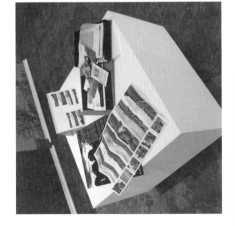

Figure 19: Photographs of SueAnne Ware's completion exhibition

for a 20-year period, the PhD was a very conscious way to build again, to make more things and to reinvigorate her practice engaging memorial design in a considered reflective manner. While her practice focuses on the design of memorials, the research more broadly explores what she calls *design activism*; that is, socially-engaged design with disadvantaged communities: *With the heroin project I'd been working primarily with street sex-workers and then, prior to the Stolen Generation project, I'd been working up in the Aboriginal communities in Arnhem Land, Pitjantjatjara and Alice.* Given the sensitivity of Ware's material, one of the difficulties with her works is the time required to build relationships and to establish a trusting dialogue with her clients.

> *It might take three years just to build trust because you're talking to people who are deeply affected by things. They have to learn you're not there for self-gain, and learn how to trust you. And you actually have to learn about them as well.*

Thus the three projects that emerged from the research – the Stolen Generation Memorial, the Memorial to Victims of Heroin Overdose, and the Road-as-Shrine – were prefaced by establishing networks and relationships with communities and stakeholders, and developing a rich understanding of the social contexts.

The research provided space for Ware to reflect upon the complexities of her work: its extended processes, politics and non-traditional relationship to landscape architecture. A critical discovery was the importance of process and what constituted that process.

> *One of my realisations was that I'm just as interested in process as I am in product…and particularly the process of engagement. I had all the interviews with the people that worked on the heroin memorial; I kept collecting all these letters during it. Then there was the process of the project changing over time – it's about landscape, which is also a process of becoming! And memory is also a process. How people remember changes. Whereas before the PhD, I would have said, "No, I'm a designer, you design what you design and put it out there in the world and you look at how people respond to it."*

The research also revealed to Ware that the pragmatic processes of engaging with councils and clients and the direct processes of dealing with the landscape – the ground-proper – were equally valuable parts of her work.

> *These processes of engagement were so much more than I'd thought. I didn't realise how much process this work had until the final project. You do these things and work with these people over a period of time, but how conscious you are of it at the time is less clear. This PhD forced me to ask, "Well, hang on,*

how did I make that decision? Where did that come from?" And then, "Oh yeah, because of three years of fighting over whether it's going to be red or pink!"

While the meta-questions around temporality, ephemerality and memorials mostly stayed the same, questions of whom and of what was memorialised became incredibly important:

It's quite obvious to do a memorial to the Stolen Generation – everyone's not happy about that issue – but the heroin one as well as the Road-as-Shrine was more difficult. Australian society is, and will always be, ready to apologise for the Stolen Generation, whereas heroin addicts and overdose victims aren't necessarily seen as victims... There are huge ethical issues with this kind of work. You're dealing with live people and their stories. Talking about it as an academic and gaining your academic brownie-points sometimes feels exploitative. Those kinds of moral-ethical dilemmas hit me in the face all the time. Each project had moments where, all of a sudden, I'd question what the hell I was doing, in addition to the 'what, why and how'. How am I working with this community, with these clients?

Ware regards the basic premise of her work – the relationships *between landscape and memories that are both emerging and shifting* – as straightforward; however, these concerns became difficult when working with the traditionally static nature of memorials. Through the Heroin project that became part of the Melbourne Festival, Ware found ways to bring in other voices and techniques of street art and of art practices as a way to rethink these traditional memorial ideas. These questions and the preoccupation with memory and death were what led her to structure the PhD research catalogue using three voices.

I said, "Okay, I'm going to tell stories, and I'm going to talk about my own memories, because it's my way into this, like why the hell am I interested in death, and why the hell am I interested in memory and landscape?" So the front piece of every chapter is my own stories, starting with my aunties and some of our practices and voodoo and what that means in terms of memory, but also what memorials are to them and how they made me who I am...

Ware's practice of making is diverse, incorporating several media. In addition to some of the more conventional techniques of drawing, mapping, planting and groundwork, Ware has made idiosyncratic maquettes throughout her career that are not obviously related to landscape issues. These, which she calls her *kooky-kitsch-making-practice*, sit rather uncomfortably within the academic context of the work; however, they were her way of solving design problems: *They were a memory-trigger for me.* The PhD gave her the confidence to pull that material into the research and to discuss what she realised was an important part of her practice: *When you start looking through the exegetic text, it moves from my own personal memories, to the markings on my body, to these memory practices.* Those practices within the personal narrative section serve as another way to introduce and frame the overarching research themes.

The research process allowed Ware to reflect on issues of authorship and her practice. The question of *how heavy the hand of the designer is* has also been critical, since the Berkeley emphasis is on community participation and the role of designer as facilitator rather than as sole author. Whilst she questions such a complete handing-over of the design, she is also aware with projects as sensitive as hers of not wanting to over-design or to over-write other people's voices:

> *The Stolen Generation was about having multiple designers, multiple voices, and then my curating that, writing a brief, and working with members of the Stolen Generation; whereas the heroin memorial was much more about my hand as a designer, but trying to tell and communicate other people's reflections about it - for example, people who had lost someone to an overdose.*

Perhaps one of the most significant realisations for Ware was that her design work could be located within the discourse of landscape architecture while also being projected as a catalyst for social change.

> *I don't think I would have ever owned up before the PhD. It's really daggy to call yourself a design activist…it took a PhD to go, "Yep, I don't care, that's what I am!" I know that the work and my questioning of how heavy my hand should be still continues, but until the PhD that question wasn't as conscious.*

Although her work doesn't fit neatly into normative landscape architecture, the PhD revealed that she draws heavily from landscape architectural practice as well as art and architecture.

> *It was really empowering to come back to my own discipline and say, "Yeah, I know a lot about landscape architecture." And although my work's always had a social aspect to it, I wouldn't have been as upfront about saying, "I don't really give a shit; I'm going to do something that's about social engagement."*

Her clients have also benefited from the PhD since the research has produced a strong body of work that she can use to demonstrate her processes and the unique manner of client engagement.

RICHARD BLYTHE

A TERROIR OF TERROIR (OR, A BRIEF
HISTORY OF DESIGN PLACES)
COMPLETED: 2008

Richard Blythe is Professor and
Dean, College of Architecture and
Urban Studies, Virginia Tech and
a founding director or TERROIR.
Richard was the former Dean of the
School of Architecture and Design
at RMIT University.

*Understanding how reflective practice usually works, as
opposed to how people assume it works, is very difficult. As a
candidate I discovered, and now as a supervisor I recognise in
the work of others, that finding an appropriate and original
'voice' for the work is a difficult and essential component
of the research. A big part of the PhD is discovering this
'voice' - and how it is that you're a design practitioner in the
world and what your unique position is, because that is your
contribution.*

Professor Richard Blythe, Head of RMIT's School of Architecture and
Design, began postgraduate study without any intention of becoming an
academic. Rather, he undertook this study in order to specifically address
educational *gaps* and, more importantly, to reconcile his creative interests in
poetry and sculpture with the reality of architectural practice.

Following a *very technical* undergraduate education at the University
of Tasmania, Blythe became a sessional and then part-time teacher at the
University, and was actively involved in the local architectural discourse on
place-making and the Tasmanian landscape. This early teaching experience first
revealed that he had a natural ability with theory, and also suggested to him
that there might be a way to combine his poetic-philosophical interests with his
interest in architecture.

Looking to refine his academic skills, to *teach myself how I thought
research worked*, Blythe completed a Master's in architectural history at the
University of Melbourne that looked at the work of his architect grandfather Sydney
Wallace Thomas Blythe. Following this, his academic profile expanded rapidly:

*I just went 'Whoosh!' with a whole bunch of writing in journals
that dealt with the way we construct space - the politics and
aesthetics of space. I worked with the issues of wilderness
in Tasmanian space - partly out of interest, but also trying*

to imagine what kind of PhD done from Tasmania might have international relevance.

By the time he enrolled in his PhD thesis with Dr John Macarthur at the University of Queensland in 1996, he was able to articulate more clearly his interest in an architecture that engaged poetics, the landscape and the way people occupy the world, and then at *how these things related through the arrangement of the object world. I tried to work out how you would structure a PhD around that...but I hadn't understood that there was an option to do it by designing things.*

In 2000, Blythe set up his architectural practice TERROIR with Gerard Reinmuth and Scott Balmforth, and was finding it increasingly difficult to meet the added demands of writing a PhD. Significantly, Reinmuth and Balmforth had just enrolled in the Invitational Program of design practice research at RMIT with Professor Leon van Schaik. It was then that he really became aware that he could do his PhD alongside Reinmuth and Balmforth. He soon changed enrolment to RMIT's PhD by Design Practice Research, supervised by van Schaik, with whom he had previously collaborated in devising the design research policy of the Royal Australian Institute of Architects and in studio teaching at the University of Tasmania.

It was fantastic, because instantly it brought the inquiry back within the interests of the practice and it meant that my whole PhD was about what was going on in the office. That whole inquiry was strengthened by having a PhD that grows out of design projects that you're doing, rather than one that is structured around reading the life-works of the theorist who is currently in favour.

The shift was initially difficult for Blythe. Having spent several years researching through writing and reading, Blythe needed to return his focus to his own and to TERROIR's design practice. What were their processes? How and what did they design?

This was a big change to the very academic writing about landscapes I had been doing, all very external to design...then all of a sudden there was this need to discuss the design work you're doing at the same time as dealing with those concerns. The gap between what I was doing in 'cultural theory-land' and in design research became obvious to me and it was a complete dilemma. I was trying to create the design research in the same way. What I now realise is that, of course, all research begins with very close observation of the world and, out of that close observation, you notice some inconsistencies or gaps. In design research, what you're observing is the design itself and the design's engagement with the world. I hadn't got that at all; none of us really had.

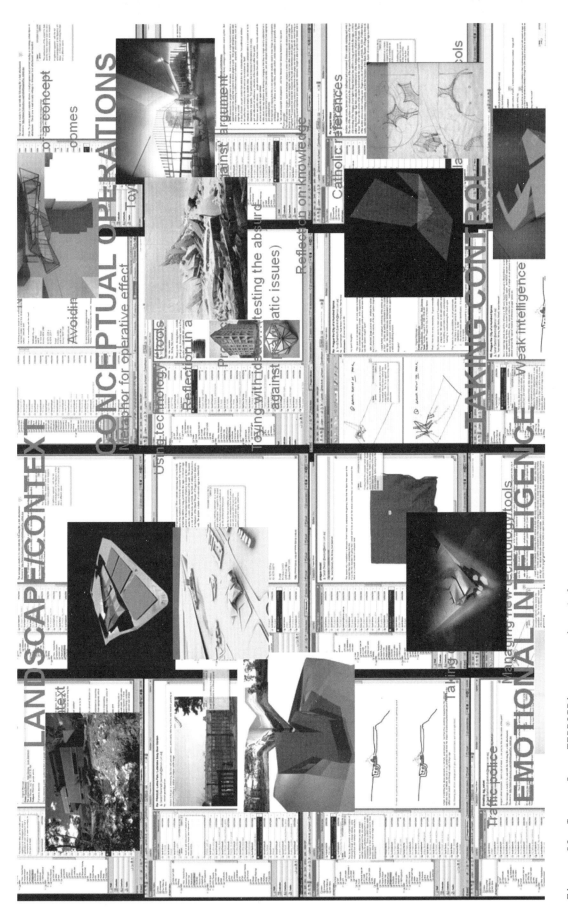

Figure 20: Image from TERROIR's research catalogue

One of the questions addressed at this early stage was Blythe's longstanding interest in landscape and particularly in the *Tasmanian wilderness*, where he had been exploring issues of landscape through a Tasmanian urban park in order to investigate the formation of an unplanned colonial city and what this reveals about the views and attitudes of the people in that landscape. Then, as he recalls, he was challenged to reflect on his motivations:

> *All of a sudden, that conversation was broadened very quickly to why that question of wilderness was important to me, as someone operating out of that space. If you used Leon's words it would be: "What's the spatial intelligence at work" in the way that we're designing? Why am I so driven by the question of landscape - a question that preceded my architecture? There was obviously something going on there. We all realised we had quite a different way of looking at landscape from some of our colleagues in Sydney, who had a very Romantic view...*

Discussions at the following Research Symposium events and then between the three partners clarified their take on landscape and its role in making architecture in particular and personal ways. Having grown up during the Tasmanian dams debates, and particularly the Gordon-below-Franklin Dam project, Blythe recalls, *Everyone had to have a position on the landscape. You couldn't lean on the fence. We began to see those spaces and the landscape as highly political, constructed politically; the wilderness in Tasmania didn't exist prior to 1979. In this process they were essentially pulling apart what we were taught in Architecture school, which was 'site analysis' and the checklist of eight things that you looked at; for we could see an infinite number of things that go into constructing people's relationship to the landscape... So how do you make places that engage people?*

From this they outlined three definite strands to their practice. The first concerned spatial psychoanalysis, *the personal engagement with the object world and the sensory and memory relationship with place;* the second acknowledged *the political construct of social relationships to place and objects,* which explained their interest in how the things that they made related to the social body; and the third adopted *the* 'constructivist thread' *or the construction of meaning through the experiences of those things.* As Blythe further explains:

> *When we're designing, we're talking about the possibilities of interaction and what people might be seeing and feeling. We try to draw those as part of the drawing-out of that object...Those three strands are really embedded through what TERROIR's done right from the beginning, but it only became clear at that point in the PhD. This moved us on from a concern with wilderness*

to being concerned with any kind of spatial construction including urban environments.

TERROIR's Peppermint Bay project (Hobart, 2005) had just been completed as Blythe began his RMIT PhD, so it became a significant point of reflection. Blythe returned to the project at least three times and, interestingly, saw it in an entirely different way each time:

> *Peppermint Bay becomes a really nice measure to explain how the thinking changes…At the beginning, we were talking about Francis Bacon's essay 'Of Gardens' and his discussion of a spatial landscape structure, and how this linked into our own thinkings about psychology of space. Next, there were our observations of how the structure of the place works and how that becomes condensed within the building. Finally, we came back to thinking about the sensibility of that object read in its vast landscape. How do you create an iconic building in a landscape that's five kilometres from ridgeline to ridgeline? Our response was to create a powerful internal experience. We just played the thing right down to the point of almost making it unattractive… we tried to force the thing to make sense once you were in it. And from the interior you re-read the entire landscape in a different way.*

As a result, this project became an invaluable precedent for explaining their work to future clients, including an important but unbuilt project in China, where the language differences required a very careful and precise explanation of TERROIR's design methodology and work to date. Through these discussions in China, other threads about the work opened up, giving Blythe further opportunities *to see Peppermint Bay in a completely new way.* One such discovery was TERROIR's working between exterior and interior:

> *We were doing it intuitively. It's like the Little Prince story where someone asks the Little Prince, "Is that image a drawing of a hat?" and he says, "No, it's a snake with an elephant inside." This is the story of our buildings. I tried to unravel what we're doing in making that surprise, what it is about the wondrous moment when you discover that, within that blunt object, there's a special moment in there and things are slightly skewed…and doing so allows people to see something about the place not otherwise apparent.*

These discoveries led Blythe to understand how observation and reflection work together to enhance the design process:

> *Designers reflect by designing more things. The reflection happens in the next design project, not necessarily in the*

writing about the previous one. The Chinese project is a classic example. It wasn't my writing about Peppermint Bay; it was my going to do another project that opened up a realisation about something going on in that earlier project...it's in the close observation of designing things rather than creating a theory and then trying to apply it to a project or a practice.

During this period of absorption in the PhD, Blythe, Reinmuth and Balmforth also explored their collaborative design processes, a process that made Blythe uncomfortable. *I don't draw a lot, so what is it that I do as a designer?* They discovered that their design process happens with all three working together; at the outset, Blythe talks ideas through, trying to create a conceptual framework *that doesn't describe what the building is but creates a set of rules or a space within which we can begin to explore the building.* From that point, a set of principles is established that guides the design decisions.

Then there would be this flurry of emails, exchanges and drawings - things going everywhere - and at some point I would write back something short that said, "Okay, this is what we are doing. We've talked about all these things: some we've forgotten; others have held some curiosity throughout our conversation..." And then I'd write a statement trying to get in my head what we were doing. After one Research Symposium presentation, Scott [Balmforth] said, "Ah, this is what you actually do, Richard!"

We could go back through every project and find that statement...and Scott was able to articulate that this is what makes things clear for him and Gerard, and then the project can actually start happening. When we started, we knew there was something special going on between the three of us, but there was a fear about trying to uncover authorship. What would that do? Is that destructive? But, actually, all of that disappears as you get to it...

It's a very hard thing to explain, but the positive part is developing complete confidence in what you do as part of that team. At the end of it I was far more confident that I was doing something that, a) was designing, and b) was valuable and useful on an ongoing basis.

MARTYN HOOK

THE ACT OF REFLECTIVE PRACTICE:
THE EMERGENCE OF IREDALE
PEDERSEN HOOK ARCHITECTS
COMPLETED: 2008

Martyn Hook is a Professor of
Architecture, Deputy Pro Vice-
Chancellor Partnerships of the
College of Design and Social
Context (DSC) and Dean of the
School of Architecture and Urban
Design at RMIT University. He
maintains his role as Director
of multi-award winning iredale
pedersen hook architects, a studio
practice based in Melbourne and
Perth, dedicated to appropriate
design of effective sustainable
buildings with a responsible
environmental and social agenda.

You can talk and talk and talk and try to be academic, but the real value in the reflective practice process is just doing what it is you do and thinking about what it is you do and how it is you do it. It's not about trying to transform the way that you do things; it's about trying to transform the way that you think about what it is you do. And through that thought process, the work becomes transformative, anyway.

Associate Professor and one of the three directors of iredale pedersen hook architects, Martyn Hook enrolled in a design practice research PhD at RMIT in 1998. At that stage, the Bristol-born Hook had been in Melbourne for two years working as a full-time academic at RMIT. Hook, whose family migrated to Perth, WA, in 1981, completed his undergraduate architecture education at Curtin University. Following a period with local Perth firm Donaldson + Warn Architects and teaching at UWA's and Curtin University's architecture programs, Hook left Australia in 1993 for the Bartlett School of Architecture to undertake a Master's under the direct supervision of Sir Peter Cook, which he completed in 1994. His undergraduate education (with modernist scholar Duncan Richards and English immigrant and Architectural Association alumnus Bill Busfield), his Master's and then his work with Donaldson + Warn Architects and their investment in European functionalism and the local culture of Perth, provided a diverse beginning to Hook's career and one that would see him pursue the pragmatism of those modernist influences but also the AA-inspired fascination with diagrams, constraints and the visible and invisible systems of the city.

iph had not yet begun when Hook first arrived at RMIT, and at that stage his teaching and PhD research were concerned with the content of his Bartlett Master's: *ideas of constraint, chance and dimension that, at that point, applied much more to strategies of urban planning than anything else.* Hook was also increasingly involved with small architectural jobs, warehouse conversions, backyard renovations and café fit-outs. At this time he also became involved in architectural journalism and critique, which culminated in his role as Melbourne editor of Monument Magazine from 1998 to 2000 and then associate editor until 2007. It was in the midst of this in 1999, one year after his PhD enrolment, that Hook and his two long-standing friends Finn Pedersen and Adrian Iredale decided to pitch for a job designing an orangutan enclosure for the Perth Zoo. Much to their surprise, they won, and thus began the practice of iredale pedersen hook: *at that point, things got a little bit divergent!* From this point onwards, Hook's research, teaching and practice became conceptually difficult to reconcile.

> *The practice was going off in a completely different line, primarily because of the association with two other individuals and the way this association was actually altering the way that I was practising. Simply through the divergent paths of the other two, things would change and were slightly different. They were immediate influences that to that point had just been overt or oblique.*

At this time, Hook's career *across all its facets* was moving at a rapid pace and it became increasingly difficult to re-engage with his PhD in its original incarnation. Whilst he spoke about the work in the terms of his previous ideas of constraint and chance, people and critics could see that there were other things going on in the work, *something to do with these two other blokes I was in practice with! I was kind of denying the existence of other influences that were beginning to push in onto the work.* At that stage, Hook was torn between what he perceived as a PhD engaged in reflective practice being about *his own* work, and his work as a part of iph. At this time, too, and amplifying this disjunction, Iredale and Pedersen both enrolled in the Invitational Program of design practice research under the supervision of Professor Leon van Schaik. Because of his close involvement with them, Hook began to lay bare his own role within the practice: *Through that process of helping them be more articulate about what it was they were trying to do, I began to actually reveal much more about what I was trying to do within my own work.*

This moment of realisation occurred during what Hook remembers as a *nightmarish* Research Symposium review in 2004 with Ranulph Glanville and Jonathan Hill.

> *I was completely under the pump and I just blew it, totally blew it. I was late, the computer wouldn't work, there were about 50 people jammed in Leon's office watching it because they couldn't get a projector somewhere else. Ranulph tore me to shreds and said, "You're talking about all this stuff, but what about the other things that are in the work?" and I just couldn't answer what the other things in the work were, but of course the other things in the work were basically the other two partners and*

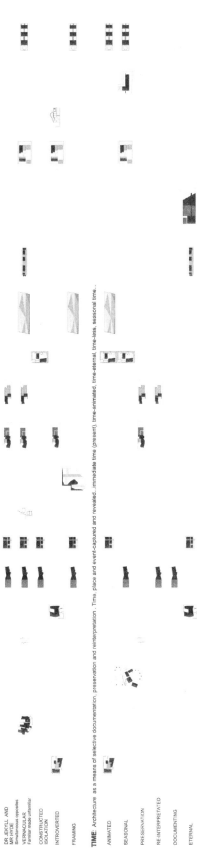

Figure 21: Image from iph's research catalogues

the manner in which the other partners were inflecting on what it was that I was doing, and how that process had occurred over a number of years to arrive at that point.

Following that event – and a heavy night of drinking with the other two partners – Hook realised that the only way forward was to rejoin the practice within the PhD project, *and it was at that moment that the design practice research became a project for the office.* From then on, the research of each practitioner stopped being three independent projects and became one collaborative work. All three presented together at the Research Symposium reviews and would also work together to produce the presentation. *Then everyone who was looking at this thing was able to understand the way that these things operated together. The process then became for Hook an entirely different thing: It became enjoyable, completely unlaborious. It became fascinating, it became like we were working on a competition together. The debates were both internal within the practice and also external in the way in which we then communicated what the practice was about.*

This *ditching of the old PhD* and embarking on a new direction was Hook's first seminal PhD moment. From then on, Hook began to unpack what was his role within the practice as well as with the other two, trying to define what the practice was and how it operated. As he recalls, this process shifted the entire flavour of all three practitioners' research:

There were things they then didn't have to say because I was saying it and therefore it allowed them to focus on their discrete bits within the practice. So Finn was allowed to focus on his agenda of indigenous housing and working in indigenous communities and Adrian was allowed to focus on these kinds of devices he played with in order to do backyard renos which then became houses. My role started to actually be about, "Why does Finn do what he does? And why does Adrian do what he does? And why do I do what I do? And how does all of that stuff then start to come together?"

At this same time, iph was invited to contribute a pavilion to the Pavilions for New Architecture exhibition held at Monash University in 2005. This project, one of Hook's last that began with the idea of material constraint, became another important moment where the research direction expanded. The project began with the premise of creating space by the most minimal, economic and sustainable means and consisted of six sheets of 1200x2500 plywood used to construct the pavilion with five designed brackets that held the sheets in a very particular manner. But as Hook recalls,

What really came out of that project were the questions, "Why would you bother doing this?" and, "How does that become

useful?" While there was a level of poetry and dexterity to
it, there was also an understanding that the study could
be expanded: "If we took on this agenda about a minimum
of means to create architecture, what then are the social
material ramifications of that?" ... "Well, you can re-use the
bits of plywood. It becomes adaptable - you could take these
brackets in a bag on a plane and go and make another enclosure
somewhere else. You could scale it up or scale it down." So then
it became, "Where is the architecture? Is the architecture in
the assemblage or is the architecture in the bracket? Or is the
architecture in the idea?" There was a clear point through this
tiny project that actually started to say, "Well, this is one idea
about research into the 'fetishisation' of constraint and then
this is one notion about what that identification might lead to."
I think it was a very key departure point.

That project then developed and became part of the *New Trends in Architecture* exhibition in 2006. Out of that emerged an idea of how all three directors could discuss the work of the practice in spatial terms, *both through the figure of the plan* but also expressing the generosity within the work through that ability to be reconfigured. This *New Trends* model – a box of plywood with inserts in it – became an idea about adaptability that evolved from the New Pavilions project: *You could reconfigure it and, as this exhibition was sent around the world, you could say to people, "Well, you do what you like and you reconfigure this object as you choose."*

This new research direction was less about Hook's own work but more actively about the practice and how iph produced such divergent work depending, as Hook says, *on who was driving the bus or who took the lead on the project.* This shift in focus and the *unpacking* of how the practice came to be ironically involved a closer look at each practitioner as individuals. Hook, along with Iredale and Pedersen, looked to articulate the collective value system, both personally and professionally, and then the way those three value systems combined to form the agendas through which iph pursued their architecture.

The first expression of this process was the production of a conical diagram that described iph's tri-polar agenda with its three different personalities, each with particular skills and bias that came together to form the *object* of iph. Having stated this, however, and *collectively establishing a cohesive manner that the practice began to work in, it became less about the individuals and much more about what the practice was.* From this, Hook then identified a eld *of concerns* represented by a circle with five fields (social sustainability, re-calibrating the suburbs, referential landscape, environmental construct, and means of economy) located equidistant about the perimeter. This field of concerns was not only what all three believed underpinned the work but was also the way in which the work was produced. As Hook says:

This became about trying to communicate, not a quantitative assessment of the work, whether "it's good or bad," but, "What is it we're trying to achieve in this practice?" and "Which of the projects are meeting those expectations and which of the projects aren't?" So then it re-introduced this notion of the collective value system as a device by which you might say, "Well, look, guys. We know this project is good. But why is it good? Is it good because it meets the client's expectations or it was on budget or on time, or is it good for another reason?" The PhD was really about trying to say, "How can we objectively begin to look at these projects and reflect not only on why we think they performed in a particular way, but also why we're happy with them?"

At this point, Hook's research was also affecting the other practitioners and the very characteristics of their design. While each partner had begun by mapping their projects in very particular ways, identifying the particularities of each director's hand, Hook then shifted this investigation by saying, *Well, yeah, OK, I can do that, but actually it's more interesting if we look at something else beyond that.* Once they established the *field of concerns and ideas of speculations,* an element of hybridity evolved within the work and, interestingly, authorship became much less obvious. As Hook explains, *I'm not just talking about a plan form. It might be the manner in which material is treated or how a particular detail has evolved. That idea of the hybridity resulting from the reflective practice is more interesting than the origin of who did what to start with. Saying that you're a field and not a three-poled cone implies much more integration.* Hook points out that, following their completion seminar, there is now a recognised consistency in the partners' architectural language and the dialogue between them. They use the *fields of concerns, as he says, in the way we sit down with a project and say, "Where does it fit? What's missing on this thing? How do we up the social agenda?"*

The impact of their design practice research for all of iph has been considerable and far-reaching. A more focused direction emerged that reflects more strategically which projects they seek to do and then how they go about doing them. Whilst they began very interested in housing, they are now far more concerned with broader community-based projects that have a greater social or public impact. As Hook says,

Through the reflective practice process what emerged is a concern for ideas about community: how can you do things that really raise the agenda of modernism's contribution to society? How can the architect use their forces for good? It was a clear modernist project: how might architecture improve people's lives? And we're part of a generation that's returning to those agendas…the social parameters of the modernist project have returned and it's now about, "How do we fix social housing? How do we provide spaces that are good in a community construct? How do we produce buildings that look good and are durable? How do we engage with ecological systems and not destroy things simply because we're creating something?" I think all of those things are very old ideas and they've only now kind of come back into the forefront. There's a resurgence of the idea that intelligent architecture can actually contribute to society and architects can be more valued than they currently are.

This has also carried through into Hook's teaching and academic work, where design studios are engaged with real problems and projects. For example, the *Think Brick* design projects look specifically at the utilisation of brick as a material applied to social housing, a library or a school, and his technology seminars explore mass housing that utilises industrial concrete systems or prefabrication as a solution. *The studios take on more of a social agenda: how might the value in a place be drawn out through a process? Now I think it's more useful to use the design studio as an act of speculation around real problems rather than more fanciful ones.*

I think going through the reflective practice process has really been about saying, "If these are the value systems that are present in practice, how might I then begin to understand how those value systems become present in academia? How might my work as a critic begin to address some of those concerns?" That awareness addresses the notion of the integrative nature of practice and academic scholarship, and the way the values of practice become integrated into the academy and then into critique and then vice versa.

(I) THE INTELLIGENT BUILDING: ARCHITECTURE AS INDUSTRIAL DESIGN
COMPLETED: 1991

(II) ZUKUNFTSMUSIK: PROTOTYPING THE TECHNOLOGICAL AND SOCIAL CONSTRUCTION OF SPACE
COMPLETED: 2008

Michael Trudgeon is a trans-disciplinary designer and architect, and Principal Designer with Crowd Productions. He has over two decades' experience in industrial design, architecture and media design. His focus is on research in new technologies and industrial design for architecture to create powerful new customer experiences. Recent projects include the concept-store design for the National Australia Bank, flagship cinema complexes at Melbourne Central and Blacktown for Hoyts Corporation, and Digital Cinema capsules for the Australian Centre for the Moving Image.

We began by seeing design as a bridge between culture, people, society and technology, and my Master's then PhD were pivotal for that research. You can develop responses that are not specifically building-based where you identify processes and map those out as a kind of network. We want to provide solutions perfectly attuned to the organism that is the organisation.

Following several years of practice and research into relationships between technology, design and culture, Michael Trudgeon, director of Crowd Productions, began his design practice research in 1990 in the first cohort of the Invitational Program. A trans-disciplinary firm, Crowd Productions is a network of designers and consultants who explore ideas, materials and technologies through design. The firm is emergent, a territory of *crowds, business expertise and methodologies* in which, using actor network theory, the client is viewed as an extended system. Rather than provide buildings *per se*, they see their work as *product service system design*, which includes design of buildings, or business propositions, or strategies to address a client's communication, human resource or technology infrastructure needs. Structured more like a film company than a typical architecture firm, Crowd Productions is thus an explicit rethinking of architectural practice.

Prior to the invitation to undertake the research, Trudgeon, an architecture graduate, had studied industrial design at the winter schools of the Domus Academy in Italy and had then participated in the major technology and culture exhibition *Deus ex Machina* (1989). At the Domus Academy the industrial design teachers were all architects and their engagement with new technologies offered Trudgeon a set of unprecedented opportunities to reconceive architecture and architectural practice.

It became clear that being able to invoke new solutions that could really enable greater fluidity and user control required being able to draw from an enormous, emerging and fluid body of

Figure 22: Image from Michael Trudgeon's research catalogue

technology and practice. Leon arrived at absolutely the perfect moment for me and so I began my research about reframing architecture as a much more fluid product with appliance modality. It became a catalyst. I needed a project to do it in and Leon literally presented that project. The research took other thinking and embedded it into what is essentially an architectural frame. And that work became a platform that then propelled the practice forward.

Trudgeon found these early attempts to bridge the two separate cultures of spatial construction and product design very exciting, yet problematic. His first solution was to imagine architecture as industrial design. This conceptual shift revealed that other disciplines could be drawn upon and brought into his evolving model and so, in addition to cinema, theatre and market research also became relevant. Trudgeon marks this as the critical moment when *the bridging, the 'trans-' aspect became essential to visualising what was going on* and he then began to completely re-imagine what space might be. Through his research, he essentially created a tool kit that described architecture as a series of elements or products. These *territories* included structure, dynamic surfaces and mechanical systems.

The overarching mentality was that if architecture today is in fact modular – the brick, the pre-fabricated window frame, etc. – there's nothing in contemporary architectural practice that optimises the opportunities modularity can deliver. If we assert that architecture is a kind of Lego system, and invest an enormous amount of effort in those modules, we then can look at the whole idea of how to assemble them. It's like the USB now on cameras or digital recorders – it's all about the connectivity, the connections. The connectivity is central and that idea is what the research ultimately delivered.

The academy, as Trudgeon calls it, delivered a coherent framework for reflection that commercial practice could not. This coincided with the realisation that the way he wanted to practise was more complex than he had imagined, and required a structure within which to research, experiment and reflect. It was thus the PhD by design practice research that provided Trudgeon with that framework. From the time he began, *the work unfolded in parallel between the built work, the technological prototyping, teaching, and the processes; so our practice literally evolved from a technology practice to an anthropological practice, but using academy methodology as a way of framing and testing. Subtitled Zukunftsmusik, which means 'Future Dreaming'*, the PhD research was an investigation of the prototyping of social and technological constructions of space and extended on problems identified in the design research and then on the subsequent gaps revealed by doing that.

I had an intuitive sense of the significance of these different disciplines, processes and prototyping, and the significance of the input and the framing, but I had no way of coherently packaging that into a pattern that could be articulated. If the design practice research Master's was really a proposition about a way to work that was very much looking at the extraordinary technological opportunities that existed in fusing industrial design and architecture together, the PhD very much came out of the real difficulty of trying to implement that.

In addressing the first gap, a series of further extraordinary gaps were revealed, which in effect became the PhD. Although Crowd Productions had developed a very sophisticated way of doing technological prototyping and introducing new technology into projects, when it came to delivering these quite radical ideas to clients, the clients *just hated them.* They could work wonderfully with technicians, physical processes, and the rapid prototyping that came out of the experimental aircraft industry, but their relationship with the client had been entirely left out. It was during the presentation of a project for the Australian Centre for the Moving Image (ACMI: the second project in the PhD) which involved a *radical solution involving lots of technology*, that this realisation occurred. As Trudgeon recalls:

We presented it to 70 people – to the organisation – and they absolutely hated it! And so we had a totally new problem. Up to this point in time, our whole idea about innovation was around the technological and design innovation that could be brought to the table without the client. I was in a state of complete panic, I had to think of how we could create a way of building a bridge between the client and us.

From this emerged a key idea in Trudgeon's research: *walking the plank* – a plank with two purposes. Firstly, the plank quite literally became a communication bridge between the firm and the client. However, the plank's second and critical role was to address the fear that clients experienced from being asked to step so far outside their comfort zones by taking on these ideas. *We were asking people to go somewhere that is dangerous, and that posed for us a very significant problem: how do you hold the hands of people who you want to take on a dangerous journey? And that really became the journey of the PhD.* The issue became to expand the conversation beyond the technological people to include the client. However, addressing this and establishing this dialogue at the outset opened up a whole new set of possibilities and design opportunities.

It became very clear to us that the design process as we were now looking at it had two parts: one was defining the question, and then there was the designing of it. The learning that came from the PhD was that we needed to involve the client in that first part – in the unpacking of the question. This didn't close down the opportunities but actually expanded them dramatically. It gave us an expanded practice… and a much more radical way of working.

An example of this process taking place was during the ACMI project. Following the first *horrific* presentation, Trudgeon went back to the office where they worked to transform the project into one that would bring people together. The idea was then represented using the idea of *walking the plank, and at one point during this they said to us,* "Okay, *if we're talking about a cinema of the future, surely we should be designing a cinema where the audience can make movies as well as merely watch them?" This was an extraordinary idea!* Their design role and the brief had been dramatically expanded, and the project evolved into a more *radical proposition.*

The next tranche of work focused on strategies to draw the clients into the conversation whilst managing risk. It was then, at this critical time, that Trudgeon took the methods from their prototyping with industrial design work that allowed for innovation *and also* risk management, and applied it spatially. *Instead of purely prototyping technology, we started literally prototyping space. We made what we call theatre sets: spatial prototypes that could be made just out of cardboard boxes or they could be incredibly elaborate.* This was then applied to a project with Hoyts Cinemas, where the proposal was to radically change the spatial experience and the way facilities were used in the public areas, all within a very limited footprint. As at ACMI, they were confronted with the various stakeholders' very entrenched views.

The nationwide food and beverage hospitality unit at Hoyts were immovable in their belief that you needed a 20-metre-long food and beverage counter. It was non-negotiable. So as a result of the techniques we had begun to develop with ACMI, we said, "Fine. What we're going to do is build a full-scale food and beverage counter, out of cardboard boxes." We flew everybody in, we walked them through and we role-played: This is what it's like serving food and beverage. We had staff acting as patrons, etc. And then we said, "Okay, let's try a little experiment. What about if we halve the counter length? It's just cardboard boxes. We're not threatening anything." And so over lunch, we redesigned the counter and moved all the cardboard boxes around with our team into this far more compact model and then we said, "Okay, let's replay this." And we did and, lo and behold, they discovered that the distances they had to travel in order to service customers had suddenly got a great deal shorter, service times were a lot less, and they started saying, "I'd be a lot less tired if I had to be doing this for four hours." And through this process, we had in effect allowed them to rethink what was possible in terms of the question, how you could define it.

These techniques also drew on Trudgeon's theatre experience and his teaching with architect Peter Corrigan, *who brought his interest and experience in theatre and set design to RMIT,* and earlier with Peter King, a radical director of performance works in Australia. Techniques of improvisation, theatre direction, script interpretation and interrogation were now folded into their processes. *In a trans-disciplinary way, we'd literally co-opted all of that and applied it to writing an architectural brief. It allowed us to transform the dynamic and these became our plank techniques – these became the planks on which we and the client walked.*

The disciplines of *academy* and the design studio-teaching formed another central part to help Trudgeon clarify these processes:

The academy is a way for allowing innovation to emerge in the classroom. Discussions are intended to generate innovation on the part of the students, that is then examined and assessed in the course of taking the studio. We started using those techniques in workshops with our clients, and combining that with the prototyping was beginning to give us a set of quite coherent tools. In the end, we've ended up with about 30 individual tools that can be applied to this kind of dynamic of asking questions and then testing the possible outcomes.

They rigorously documented their outcomes and processes and fed them back to the clients to illustrate what had been happening and where it could go. They began to talk about the architecture in terms of occupation, *a kind of ecology of occupation,* and this was how questions about the project could be asked and suggested what the architecture could be. Trudgeon drew the comparison to Le Corbusier and his *promenade architecturale,* where he talks about movement through space: *To some degree we were co-opting that thinking, but instead of a space that existed, it was a space that didn't exist. We were using techniques where we were literally writing scripts and telling people, describing spaces in a way that didn't really exist and saying, "Well, this is the story. Imagine this space."*

Trudgeon's next project provided a perfect, yet intense, environment to test these ideas again. The client was the highly risk-averse National Australia Bank (NAB). However, from their research Trudgeon came to understand that one of the major problems facing traditional banks like the NAB was that the obsession with security prevented effective communication with clients. The deregulation of banking had resulted in many other companies, for example car companies, being able to sell financial products as well. *Suddenly there was enormous competition and the banks really didn't know how to rise to the occasion. It was very clear that giving the staff much more freedom, unleashing them from their glass cages, would be one way to do this. However, that requires an enormous leap of faith.* Trudgeon had sourced very sophisticated banking technology called Teller Cash Recycler machines currently used in the Bank of Scotland; however, the unions, Occupational Health and Safety and the security groups rejected outright trying to implement it.

So, using their new *tools,* Trudgeon and Crowd Productions built an entire bank set.

We used a set builder. It looked very solid and very real. It had real carpet, door handles and things, and all the technology was real. We configured new technology the bank hadn't even thought of using. We brought it in on forklifts, put it so it looked solidly set and then we ran the various staff through it. We said, "Okay, try using this bank and see how it works." It was absolutely spectacular. We were able to role-play. We had bank hold-ups; we had staff stress-analysis. We had the whole thing in here. Our process basically allowed us to propose an innovation that was completely unthinkable. And that got us across the line.

As a result, three banks built that prototype and then it was handed over to a national roll-out architectural practice and the turnover of those banks increased by 25%. It was a key moment: *The technique demonstrated itself very powerfully. What was very exciting for us was that it allowed design thinking to be embedded in the entire process. We could use design as a way to consider the very framing of the problem at the outset.*

In order to win these jobs with very large established clients and organisations, which began to come to Crowd Productions via word-of-mouth, they had to be able to offer something immediate – or a set of deliverables. But Trudgeon's clients didn't need very competent architecture: *they needed something to save their businesses and so, in pitching against very large architectural practices offering conventional architectural solutions, we were trying to get them 'on the plank' to begin with.*

> *The other thing about the walking-the-plank analogy is that you're inching forward bit by bit. So we said, "You don't have to walk to the end. Every step we will write you a deliverable. So if you decide you want to walk back in after three steps, you won't have wasted your money. You've got a series of decisions you can make." This was really about unpacking what the design could deliver in a series of steps.*

As all of this was happening in the midst of Research Symposium presentations and trying to secure these jobs, Trudgeon had no clarity about what the final design outcomes for these projects were. They were on the plank, too. As he recalls,

> *It was emergent! I was doing a PhD at exactly the same time as evolving a kind of crisis management – we called our clients 'clients in crisis' because that was the state in which they had come to us. All we knew was that we could genuinely trust a rigorous design process if it was intelligently reflected upon: literally, taking the very PhD process itself that Leon was parlaying through the academy, and saying, "We believe in that process and at the end of the day, we believe that will deliver something that will answer the question. What we need to do is articulate that as we move as effectively as we can and demonstrate a process that is going to calm the nerves of our clients." And so it was a perfect amalgam of a kind of commercial challenge and the way in which research is recorded and reflected on within academic practice.*

Trudgeon recalls several times presenting in the Research Symposium and saying, "*At this point in time, the project is completely beyond my control." I would stand up and basically read out a series of appalling failures and absolutely kind of horrendous risks. It was very disturbing.* The PhD came together following the

NAB and at the start of the next project for the Road Transport Authority of NSW. His PhD moment was the realisation that, in fact, all of these processes they had been developing were linked, and what had shifted were the contexts:

It wasn't clear to me at the time that they were all the same process being shifted. I thought that each one was a new tool that was a unique part of a set, not a translation effectively of a single idea. In writing up the research, I realised that a number of the key factors, the radical aviation technology experiments being done by Lockheed and the dramaturgical experimentation being done by someone like Joseph Svoboda, were in fact exactly the same. Up until that point, they were remaining like a constellation of influences, not an alignment that were being drawn together by way of seeing a single idea running through them all. That was the insight and value of the PhD process.

The impact for Trudgeon has been the securing and undertaking of some extremely radical projects, another involving the NAB in an even more radical propositional idea. He states these would not have been possible without the reflective process of his research.

Without the reflection, it would not have been possible to build up an understanding of what it was we were doing, stepping back from it and see it from different angles and therefore presenting it in ways that were completely different to the way we started. That's been incredibly valuable. We've almost been able to materialise some of the thinking and the PhD as a tool that our clients can use to think about design problems and unpack assumptions about the questions they're asking. The role of the designer then is not to provide a template for solutions, but rather to be a catalyst that initiates conversation, creates the appropriate kind of hearths, campsites and fireplaces around which that conversation occurs. The designer harvests the results, testing and reflecting. Once agreed upon, the designer can then take that material to produce the appropriate outcome, whatever that may be.

(I) ARCHITECTURE IN THE
EXPANDED FIELD
COMPLETED: 1999

(II) A SEARCH FOR
COMMON PLEASURES:
CURATING THE CITY
COMPLETED: 2009

Sand Helsel is Professor of
Architecture at RMIT. Her design
research practice ranges in scale
from urban installations to urban
design. The Asian city is the
current focus of her international
lectures, conferences,
publications, exhibitions and
design workshops. She co-directs
the postgraduate research stream
X_Field, which crosses the
disciplines of art, architecture,
and landscape and urban design.

New York-born Professor of Architecture at RMIT, Sand Helsel lived in the UK for 17 years, completing her undergraduate architectural degree at the Architectural Association (AA) in London (1981) and establishing her practice and teaching at the AA. She came to Australia in 1993 to begin her newly-appointed role as Head of Architecture at RMIT. It was then that she enrolled in the RMIT design research Invitational Program. Helsel cites her undergraduate studies under the leadership of David Greene, *who taught me everything I know*, and then her design teaching at the AA as the formative years in establishing her research direction.

It was at the AA, teaching with Will Alsop and established artist Bruce McLean, that Helsel began her cross-disciplinary practice. Alsop, who had spent time in Australia, was also Helsel's introduction to RMIT and drew her attention to the country's vast scale. A two-hour drive from one side of Melbourne to the other, crossing through a relatively homogenous population and landscape, was then compared to an equivalent drive from London that involved passing through two major cities, and villages and farmland. Helsel found these differences in the cross-section and the extremes of scales very intriguing. Several of the units she taught at the AA involved road trips and exploring issues of utility and agency and then mapping different situations and transposing that information onto another site. One trip in particular, travelling across the southwest of America, took her students to land art installations including Michael Heizer's 'Double Negative' and Walter De Maria's 'Lightning Field', and then, more importantly, to large industrial installations including the 'Very Large Array' (radio telescopes) in New Mexico and the wind turbines and solar collectors outside Palm Springs, *all huge, huge landmarks that really spoke about the nature of the landscape*.

During this prolific teaching period and on another study tour, this time in Hong Kong where she met Leon van Schaik in a joint workshop between the AA and RMIT, Helsel developed her repertoire of mapping techniques, *understanding big things and really expanding the field of what architecture could be and the scale of a project*. During this Hong Kong workshop, her fascination with the Asian city began:

Figure 23: Image from Sand Helsel's research catalogue

It was the first time I'd been in Asia and I thought it was fantastic. People always ask me, "How do you compare London to New York?" and it's like, "You don't." But I could compare Hong Kong to New York. And that was one of the reasons why I decided to take on the RMIT job. Another was the landscape: Australia was the sort of place where I had a hunch that my practice would begin again in a polemical way, as opposed to my London work. And then, also, I was really interested in this geopolitical shift to the Asia-Pacific region.

This invitation to RMIT came at a critical point, *that 10-year period after you finish school, when I was really interested to do some sort of reflection, some new work, and get re-energised, and I think that 10 years is a really good point.* Following a five-year stint at the AA, she then had *an epiphany in the south of France, lying on the south-facing stone wall of a philosopher friend's rundown fifteenth-century château, and he said in French, "Oh, the sky is much too big. It frightens me." And I answer back in American, "It's lookin' a bit like a pudding bowl to me!" and I realised that it was all too perfect. You know, the cypress tree in the clearing was too well-placed. I realised I needed to get out of Europe. I needed the infinite horizon...or the infinite grid of the US. I didn't really know about the big sky in Australia, so when the opportunity came up, I took it.*

The two projects that Helsel considered the *built outcomes* of her Master's design practice research were 'Atlas', an installation that was her successful entry into the Ruins of the Future competition (1996) for the Adelaide Festival, curated by Leon van Schaik, and then her installation 'The *Freeway Recon gured*', a cross-disciplinary collaborative project. From this and from the research catalogue for her first engagement in design practice research, a pamphlet titled *99 Postcards*, she established several conclusions about her practice. Firstly, the questions relevant to architecture could be posed in other disciplines and, more particularly, the methods and concerns of the land artists outlined in *99 Postcards* were central to her practice and research. This moment of clarity occurred right at the end while planning her completion exhibition. Working out the links between projects and how she was going to move through the reflection of the work, she realised that something was missing. What began as a solution to fill a vertical gap in the room became a 10,000-word book on land art and her practice.

> *I needed something spatially, but I needed that content. I'd been showing land art slides for 20 years, but I hadn't really figured out why they were useful. I'd talked about them in different ways, but I wrote that book, which was really about whether questions asked in another discipline can be useful – really what the research was about. In doing that, I clarified the specificity in time and place, the role of the artist or the author and the notion of scale. It identified a major gap, the land art thread which encapsulated the cross-disciplines, different ways of working, attitudes towards site, the non-formalism. It crystallised all those in my conclusion.*

From this research, Helsel articulated the importance of privileging site. She found that the landscape and its ephemeral nature was the basis for the non-formalist approach that her work asserts. As she recalls, her critique of formalism and *privileging process, whether through art practice or through Archigram or mapping, very definitely was formalised in this period.* And then from the *'Freeway Recon gured'* project, done in collaboration with a landscape architect, an urban designer, a photographer, a painter and an engineer, she clarified the importance to herself of cross-disciplinary collaboration and multiplicity of authorship: *that's where that notion of multiple voices emerges, and that shifting sense of authorship and the non-categoric, the slipperiness of how we change those roles. …I was an environmentalist, as well as an artist, as well as an architect, as well as an engineer. I could wear all those hats at the same time.*

Helsel's design practice research recommenced in 2001, was a continuation and expansion of her initial research. This, Helsel explains, *operates as a very particular critique of conventional architectural practices – orthogonal drawings, plans and sections, at 1:200 scale – and one of my major conclusions was that the architectural project exists between 1:1 and 1:100,000.* The PhD research expanded on this to become a critique of the master-plan and of the very role of the architect. Here she discovered her role as designer was more as curator than as sole author-architect. She came to understand her practice as that of *a curator of the built environment*, which she sees is an ethical position. Helsel has since recognised that this second phase of research was more intensely reflective than the first, and it revealed trajectories and influences that began in early childhood.

> *I really found doing the PhD was like psychoanalysis. I went way back to my undergraduate education, certainly influenced by David Greene, but also before that I studied Fine Arts with one of the land artists, Richard Fleischner, and I realised that there wasn't enough social engagement in fine art practice, and that I really wanted to do architecture to have a context other than a gallery. In my PhD, I have little narratives about being a five-year-old growing up on the top of a 23-storey building and watching the ships come into New York Harbour, seeing the grid and the buses and taxis that looked the same size as my toys moving across that. I'm much more conscious of all those things that have shaped me and shaped the way I look at the world.*

Helsel's research included the completion of three suites of projects. The first one included two built projects, also the result of cross-disciplinary collaborations: the Korean War Memorial (2000) and the Nurses Memorial (2001). The next series, which included 'Oranges', 'This is a Map of the World' and 'Five Walks', addressed issues of collaboration that had arisen in the Korean War Memorial project, and allowed Helsel to *find her voice* both through what she was drawn to – what she calls *the Common Pleasure within the city* – but also through her collections of ephemera from cities. In the third tranche of work, the Taipei Operations exhibition and the *Taipei Operations* book, she elaborated on her ideas of the *expanded field* and what architecture can be – and here, critically, she saw the role of *architect*. As Helsel says, *this last phase of the PhD consolidated for me my role as an architect and how I work as an author.*

One of the great things that Helsel likes about the RMIT research-through-design models is that:

> *It's not that much different to what you're doing anyway, but importantly you're required to articulate it for a public forum every six months. That formality is very useful – it gets things out of your sketchbook and your head and you have to articulate them. In those moments of reflection you take stock. The structures of making the book and making the exhibition are incredibly important, too; again they bring certain conclusions together or bring things to the fore. I do hundreds of things that I don't show people…the 'Oranges' project in the PhD was an example – I'd been doing them for 10 years. Then all of a sudden they sort of became important or I realised their value.*

Immersing herself in the PhD process brought about some unexpected realisations. During the research, Helsel had been sceptical of the *PhD Moment* – sceptical of what she perceived as an unlikely existential experience that would reveal particular insight into her research – but as she says *it did happen. And that's where I really integrated my teaching practice and lecturing and writing and all of that work together.* This occurred in 2002 in Busan (formerly Pusan) in South Korea, where she was invited to do a workshop based on her Taipei work. Although the Taipei book was not yet complete, she had been lecturing about the work. Within that workshop she gave a lecture and set a project on walking to test her 'Five Walks' projects for the Melbourne Festival (2002). As she says,

> *It was an interesting point; the Taipei book, the teaching, the walks and the Asian city were all in one space. I subtitled the lecture, 'Curating the City'. And that's when the whole notion of curation came in because I realised that's what I had been doing; my attitude towards curation is that it is a different thing from design – the step before – and that's also what I do in my teaching practice. It was really interesting. Then finishing the Taipei book, I could reinforce that, and then through the 'Five Walks' project in Melbourne I used the language of the museum and the headphones. And then again, figuring out that those things were continuing from my project '99 Postcards' and my thoughts on the role of author and what my role is. It weaved all those bits of practice together. Then I had the language to see how all these things were interconnected. And that's when I shifted into the autobiographical mode where I was charting my role.*

One of the criticisms at the end of this is, "Well, what have I built?" And there's always that niggling thing. I work in an architectural school and some people around sneer and are like, "That's not doing architecture." I think I am very definitely doing architecture or contributing to the discourse in a very positive way. But there was a long period of not really knowing what I was doing.

WHITE NOISE PANORAMA: PROCESS-
BASED ARCHITECTURAL DESIGN
COMPLETED: 2009

Professor Vivian Mitsogianni
is Associate Dean and head of
Architecture in the School of
Architecture & Urban Design,
RMIT University and a director of
M@ STUDIO architects.

Mitsogianni began her postgraduate study following a six-year period of architectural practice and intense competition work, though her interest in process-based architectural design dates back to the final years of her undergraduate study during studios undertaken with Paul Morgan. But it was in these subsequent years, very immersed in Melbourne's didactic architectural culture of design and debate, that she began more seriously exploring these emerging process-based design methods. The year she began the design practice research program coincided with her commencing a lecturer's position within the architecture department at RMIT University and then, one year later in 1999, she formed the architectural practice M@ STUDIO Architects with her long-term collaborator Dean Boothroyd.

This context of practice and then teaching design at RMIT provided the opportunity for discrete design experiments and explorations to be played out and tested within her own research. Mitsogianni's design practice research began as a Master's in 1998 and was converted to a PhD in 2001. The structure includes a substantial essay at the beginning of the research catalogue, which was critical for Mitsogianni to give a contextual framework for her inquiry. This allowed her to give an extensive critique of the international process-based design ideologies. In doing this and then locating herself within that *mode* as a practitioner and academic working from Melbourne and invested in discussions of the institution, design process and the local, she has additionally provided a very particular and insightful account of the Melbourne architectural scene of the late 1980s and 1990s. Indeed, this latter point was remarked upon by one of her examiners, North American academic and theorist Felicity Scott, as being one of the particular successes of the PhD.

Mitsogianni's interest in process-based architecture – what it could be and could provide for within contemporary architecture – was developed through her own teaching and the competition work undertaken with Boothroyd. Therefore, whilst her initial engagement with her postgraduate study was admittedly less committed, her mode of practicing – with its rhythm of design teaching and peer reflection, competition work and her engagement with the Half Time Club – was

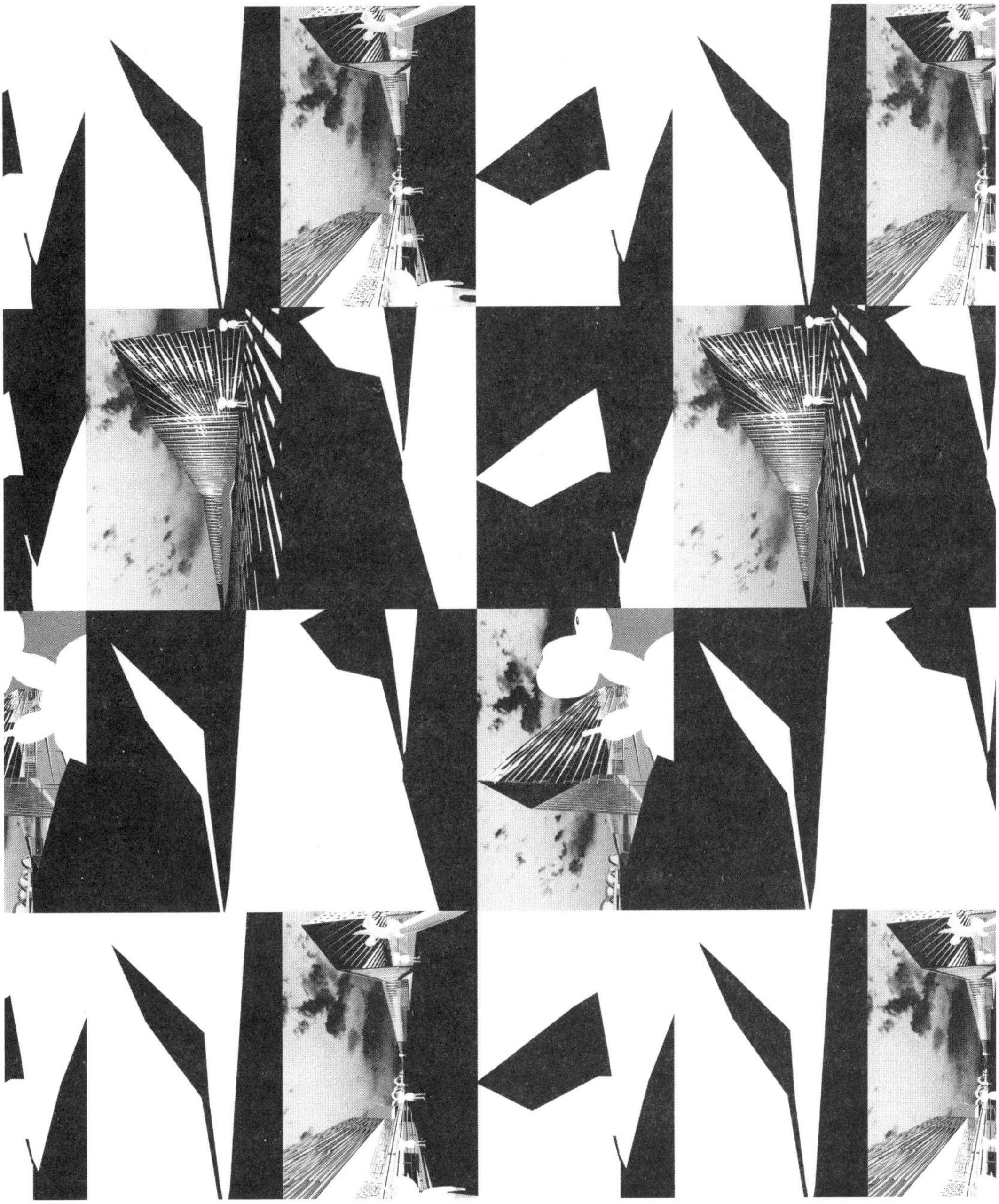

Figure 24: Image from Vivian Mitsogianni's research catalogue

by its nature reflective and structured somewhat in the manner of a PhD by design practice research: a series of cumulative and discrete design projects testing and retesting particular ideas and strategies. Importantly, it was from this work and from the overview that the role of Master of Architecture Design Studio Co-ordinator afforded that she developed an extensive critique of these ideologies and identified a series of what she felt were *problematic aspects of the field.*

Specifically, what she found problematic were the claims made for these processes, their relationship to outcome and how those processes were produced and represented. Because her own practice resided in process, this evolving critique – which found its most concise expression in the research catalogue – provided a mechanism from which to clarify her own pursuits and identify how and why they could be differentiated from the broader field.

Tracing the history of the practice and giving specific examples was partly me trying to understand my work…I'd made certain observations through doing the process-based work and through teaching and having to constantly reiterate these ideas within the environment of the design studio. I teach studios based on my own practice and so it's very difficult to communicate that practice clearly to someone else. It forces you to break it down in your head, pull out various components: how am I going to stylise this practice so someone else can understand it?

Mitsogianni was operating very clearly in research-through-design mode. The studio environment created an idealised experimental scenario in which she structured what she called *experiments* where students experimented with a process-based design approach. Parameters were built for them to work without making the methodology and intent transparent.

Mitsogianni recalls that the first stage – or tranche – of her work, culminating with her Federation Square competition undertaken with Boothroyd in 1997, was invested in process-based approaches driven primarily by formal compositional concerns: *a lot of the interest concerned composition.* As she says, it was

empowering to be able to develop things you couldn't really conceive of any other way. However, I realised during those early years I had an interest in a kind of excess of ornament, of complexity. These were things that you just couldn't draw; you couldn't sit down and draw complexity. It was incredibly empowering to be able to produce these things that were greater than you could conceive of without the process.

Parallel to this, and what began to give her work a particular and identifying characteristic, was a definite interest in Melbourne's institutional project, its status and what she saw as *its retreat into the commercial.* This aligned with her interest in local architects, including Ashton Raggatt McDougall (ARM) and Edmond & Corrigan, and their investment in the suburbs, the public project and local. Howard Raggatt's own design practice research Master's, including his 1991 Shinkenchiku Residential Competition *Another Glass House*, was particularly influential for Mitsogianni. This was work invested heavily in *technique* and process but, unlike the international process-based work she critiqued, where formal outcome was paramount, these practitioners used process as a tool to test ideas and broader issues concerning architecture, the city and the very discourse of design. Here, the final result was a by-product of ideas rather than simply a formal outcome of a very narrow sequenced diagrammatic progression. Along with the projects of Peter Corrigan, ARM's Brunswick Community Health Centre was also very influential during this period because of what Mitsogianni perceived as its role in elevating the status of the suburban institutional project. As she says, *these were buildings that punched above their weight and imbued what were very small modest buildings with a sense of the heroic.*

For Mitsogianni's work, this translated into an idea she called *reinventing the banal towards the exceptional*. The aim was to claim a presence for the public project at a *time when it was retreating into the image of the domestic. The rhetoric was de-institutionalisation and, in our projects that critique, came through as an excess of ornament. Or alternatively in the Federation Square or Mary MacKillop project, we imbued the institutional project with a level of what I called 'uncertainty'.* For her, this also differentiated the buildings from the ubiquitous large-scale-shed public institutions that adopted a very commercial vocabulary. During this period, Mitsogianni's ambition was to employ these process-based techniques into ways of contributing to local conversations.

During this time, at one of her early Research Symposium presentations, Mitsogianni's first critical realisations occurred. She had not yet realised that her concern was also vision and what she called *vision devices*, which were used to give critical distance from the process and to draw in ideas and scope for reflection. In the PhD, she traces the vision device of the prismatic lens through a number of projects. One of these, the Museum at Victoria Competition, emerged from a process that she and with her collaborators called *a Science Duck*. Simply put, it was a diagram they claimed was representative of uncertainty. In this case, however, the diagram completely informed the outcome: they simply built the diagram. During this Research Symposium presentation, Mitsogianni reflected on the difference between this approach – building the process – and subsequent projects, including Federation Square, where the idea of uncertainly *informed* process and, critically, the final result was not just a built representation of that process, but emerged from a conscious and selective translation of process and idea.

The realisation was that she wanted process to be used as leverage towards form, rather than the form being a direct facsimile of the process. *That was one of the big shifts for me: you could use a process-based approach without just necessarily building the diagram.* She remembers many discussions with her supervisor Shane Murray and also with Peter Downton – both very critical of the process movement – where she stated, "*Well, no, I'm not interested in just building the end results of the process. That's not what I do.*" As Mitsogianni identified, this was one of the key differences between her work and that of the broader *international field*.

> *What stops it from being purely mindless form is that it's imbued with certain performance criteria. It needs to contribute to questions of the institution, whether that's through program or it's about claiming difference or sometimes – as in the Mary MacKillop scheme – is about how you make a small timber visitors' centre slightly greater than itself, slightly more heroic.*

Following that period, she then looked to reflect on her own work through a critique of the international process-based design work. She followed a trajectory from Colin Rowe, through Peter Eisenman, Bernard Tschumi, the diagram practices of Ben van Berkel and then the contemporary process-based work of Greg Lynn and Ocean North, particularly as documented in a series of *Architectural Design* issues edited by Ali Raheem. Mitsogianni argued that, in the case of Eisenman's work, for example,

> *the outcomes are a result of the process alone. At a particular point, I had realised very early on in my practice, I was working on the premise that any intervention to the process was just not what you do. It was one of the primary shifts that was made and presented at an early Research Symposium just before I converted to PhD. I came to a position that the work should be developed after the process has completed. Process is just one mechanism and there was nothing really to be gained by following it doggedly through to the building.*

Mitsogianni admits she underestimated the effect that completing the PhD would have. As she says, *I assumed completing the PhD would be a formality and would make very little difference to my thinking given that by the time you finish the research catalogue you're already well over the material.* However, she discovered that the final clarity demanded by the submission and then the exhibition and having to draw together and present all research threads was, in fact, invaluable and has given her another degree of clarity.

Michael Banney, Michael Christensen, Michael Lavery, Ben Vielle: the office of m3architecture was established in Brisbane in 1997. With a significant focus on collaboration and the creative design process, m3architecture's work seeks to develop the idiosyncratic conditions of each project — including site, client, budget and brief — towards the creation of unique and project-specific outcomes, rather than uniform or formulaic buildings. The work of the practice has been recognised at both a national and international level, with numerous publications, awards and exhibitions.

The nature of reflective practice is almost a removal, an out-of-body type thing that happens where you're required to be semi-detached and then at the end of it re-join with the rest of your body. It's different to making a building, where at the end we would try to find some distance between ourselves and the building. In reflective practice, that hasn't been necessary. In fact, there's a reconnection with the material and its relationship to practice, which has absolute immediacy…our eyes have been widened to our own behaviour. –Michael Banney

The four directors of Brisbane firm m3architecture – Michael Banney, Michael Christensen, Michael Lavery and Ben Vielle – all joined the Invitational design practice research program in 2009. While each partner has a distinct voice within the research (and indeed within their practice), the project as a whole was undertaken and presented as a collective. This mode had previously been pursued by several other practices, most notably iph architects and TERROIR. As with many practitioners undertaking this design practice research, the invitation to participate occurred at the firm's ten-year mark, by which time a substantial range and depth of work had been achieved. For example, m3architecture had completed a series of small but refined buildings including the University of Queensland Micro-Health Laboratory – one of the most iconic and publicised from that period – and a significant number of larger-scale educational and research buildings. Although the practice has four partners, the office is organised as a *flat structured enterprise* that welcomes collaborative approaches from other staff members and outside practitioners. While each partner is *accountable for their own thinking*, all have been involved in a process in which the idiosyncrasies of each partner are studied and group sessions and workshops are organised for information exchange. This in many ways marks the beginning of their reflective mode of practice:

Prior to the invitation from Leon van Schaik, our process was unstructured. We're not experts in reflective practice and it's quite a complicated thing to navigate. The research provided something like the missing link. It was what we needed to get more rigour, discipline and focus into the threads that had been hanging around for a while.

During the preparation and the presentation for the first Research Symposium, they forensically revisited their existing work, looking in detail to unravel and explore their processes. This intense engagement led to the idea of developing *a type of taxonomy*. For them this held a certain objective quantitative precision, while providing a structure that surprisingly allowed for the more subjective, qualitative tendencies, processes and impulses to reveal themselves and become more *known*. That is, the laying bare of the *hard data* revealed their subjectivity and the particular hues of their work and working process. Most significantly, the taxonomy revealed to them an important and as yet unspoken truth: that the projects they found most compelling were the ones on which they collaborated as a team. This revelation became a direct way of validating their processes.

Similarly, the dozen or more categories or themes that emerged through the process of dissection by individual partners were revealed to be synonymous things or ideas, separated only by the different terminologies of each director. Through analysis, twenty categories were compressed to six, and then expanded to twelve. This process, presented at the Research Symposia, led to the further identification of subcategories, the *'for instances'* as they became known, which defined overarching themes. An example of this subtlety can be seen in two particular categories, one called *Extending Conventional Ways of Making* and the other *Lifting the Ordinary out of the Prosaic*. The first category describes a process of looking at traditional materials and traditional ways of *making* but using them in unusual or unprecedented ways. In contrast the second, *Lifting the Ordinary out of the Prosaic*, looks at extending conventional ways of making as understood with the aim of *lifting an entire environment out of its ordinariness*. For example, their brick project, the UQ Micro-Health Laboratory, takes standard brickwork convention and turns it on its head. In doing this, m3architecture addresses an array of very ordinary brick buildings through the insertion of their one project into that series. While the second category is an act of reframing tradition as well as expanding on that tradition, the first is less tied to the existing.

This process of dissection involved many hours and nights of discussion, making diagrams and writing, *a process of iteration and reiteration and then review over many weeks,* a process of narrowing the field. Whereas the first Research Symposium was a very matter-of-fact cataloguing of the work, the second, in which the idea of the taxonomy was tested, brought about the realisation that they had *very dryly tried to dissect and preserve themes and figure out consistencies between projects and between people,* which was misleading *because it was*

Figure 25: Image from m3's research catalogues

portrayed with absolute objectivity and accuracy, but was of course riddled with subjectivity, thus making it inherently inaccurate and at the wrong level of architectural discourse.

Following this Research Symposium, m3architecture became more strategic with the level of detail, looking for and presenting the political and ethical persuasions of the practice adjacent to these detail moments. In their next presentation, they returned to the taxonomy but framed these *very dry, matter-of-fact architectural techniques within a more informative or subjective context…it was a very slow-burn process!*

This process of iteration led m3architecture to a position where *almost subliminally* they came to a collective understanding of the work and the processes. At this stage, the work was embraced as a project within the office, and thus became more than just an intellectual endeavour.

One of the major breakthroughs was that moment when it was identified that we could conduct the process of our own investigation as we would any other project. In the same way that we would find the 'specificity that surprises' within a project, we'd find the specificity that surprises within our own practice. Then we felt like we owned the process and then we made great strides in being able to communicate it, first to ourselves and then to other people, in a manner that is representative not just of the way we work, but who we are.

The actual representation of this process in the final research catalogue also became a significant defining moment in its own right. Here the broader contexts are expressed as *the state of affairs*, and the design emerges through the distillation of this state of affairs into a strong concept or a loaded diagram. These two broader themes tie the four directors together, despite the subtle inflections of difference between them.

Each of us takes the lead and the responsibility in different projects, so the different colours and interests appear…not only because there are different clients and specifics of site and context but because of the peculiarities of the person who heads it up. We all recognise and draw out different things from the 'project pool' and then our own personal idiosyncrasies begin to surface in different ways. Add to that the complexity of the different project permutations and combinations of teams, and you end up with project potentials that are reasonably unpredictable.

The particular mix of personalities and interests in m3architecture found exceptional expression within the research catalogue and in the final exhibition. Approximately one-third of the research catalogue was dedicated to that found *outside of ourselves,* and the other two-thirds contained what is known to be *within ourselves,* while between them is a mediating condition where, as they suggest, *we locate the idea of useful difference.* This carried through into their final set of exhibition posters that captured the themes, the trajectories of the directors, and the overall practice within the same space. Each of the themes can be read individually, or else the overall practice can be *felt* by understanding all of these themes together.

The impact of the research for m3architecture has been significant. The collective approach that they took in the research and the assessment affirmed the essential values and strengths of their collaboration. Since the final examination, the partners have actively attempted to have as many of them as possible working on projects. There is a clear understanding that projects benefit from this collective attention, and are therefore *valued more*. As Banney reflects:

> *We now understand how each of our little pieces of the jigsaw puzzle fits into the whole. We can deploy our own idiosyncrasies more usefully and positively, whereas prior to the research process we were all a little bit aimlessly meandering. There's a subtle but important difference between being self-conscious and being self-aware. We got to the point where we could look beyond our own self-consciousness from that ego realm and into the realm of what you can know about yourself with some certainty and greater awareness. This is what we took away at the end of the process.*

The scrutiny of their peers also assisted the development of self-awareness. They describe the Research Symposium critique sessions with their *phenomenal range of panellists* as akin to looking into a mirror – albeit one *tinted with the particularities of each critic*. They came away with *a need to analyse the comments of others so we could then, in a more informed way, hold that mirror up to ourselves, and ultimately then be responsible for finding our own voice.*

In terms of their buildings and the design process, the research clarified a *working discipline* or a framework for discussion and design methodologies that can be readily drawn upon. They identified that the act of designing buildings is *somehow immersive or subversive* and they are now more able to understand the origins of an idea and then quickly identify where they might sit thematically, ethically or politically. This in turn enables clearer understanding of their decision-making, so that process lends greater confidence to the proposition. In their words, *there's a strong sense now that it's coming from a tested source.*

MAKING AND USING THE
URBAN ENVIRONMENT:
FURNITURE, STRUCTURE,
INFRASTRUCTURE
COMPLETED: 2010

Nigel Bertram established NMBW Architecture Studio in 1997. Their architectural work has been widely published and awarded across categories, from single and multiple residential design, small public works, the adaptive re-use of existing buildings for contemporary workplace and educational spaces, to peripheral urban design strategies. Nigel's research and practice explores contemporary relationships between architecture, infrastructure and landscape; the creative and opportunistic everyday use of urban environments, and the influence of local building practices and traditions.

I didn't want [the PhD] to be about me or to be a manifesto of our practice for the world...It was about particular projects: ten things that existed in the world and had validity. They were facts I didn't have to rationalise, or argue for their existence; I just had to work out a set of critical issues that could join them together – and not a comprehensive set, or not the only set of issues that might join those projects together. It's like trying to say, "Well, how can we take these facts and arrange them?" That's the difference about its being a PhD by publication – the works have already established some sort of validity. They're there. You can't argue with them and they've been published.

The late '90s and the first decade of the 21st century saw a proliferation of architects and academics pursuing new emergent practices of digital design. Process, often automated, was critical, and the buildings a splendorous display of non-standard geometries and serpentine surfaces. Adjacent to this paradigm was the development of another stream of architectural thought that resisted the ubiquity of the digital and form-making, and instead looked to the immediate urban environment, the ordinary and the everyday, as a place for exploration. The work of NMBW Architecture Studio is one such firm that works with the local and with questions of urban occupation that interfaces with vernacular types and patterns of behaviour. Thus the PhD of Nigel Bertram, one of the three directors of NMBW, not only captures a period of practice and research, but also represents one form of architectural inquiry that runs parallel to the more overt emergent architectural discourse. Bertram's research focuses on urban architecture, and investigates the ways in which precise logical decisions and actions that do not limit the meaning or interpretation of spaces encourage appropriation and active engagement in the everyday urban realm.

Along with Paul Minifie, Bertram completed a PhD by publication, one manifestation of design practice research within the Invitational Program, in

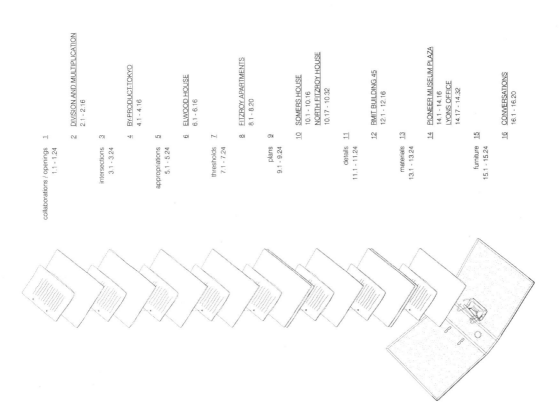

collaborations / openings 1
1.1 - 1.24

2 DIVISION AND MULTIPLICATION
2.1 - 2.16

intersections 3
3.1 - 3.24

4 BY-PRODUCT-TOKYO
4.1 - 4.16

appropriations 5
5.1 - 5.24

6 ELWOOD HOUSE
6.1 - 6.16

thresholds 7
7.1 - 7.24

8 FITZROY APARTMENTS
8.1 - 8.20

plans 9
9.1 - 9.24

10 SOMERS HOUSE
10.1 - 10.16
NORTH FITZROY HOUSE
10.17 - 10.32

details 11
11.1 - 11.24

12 RMIT BUILDING 45
12.1 - 12.16

materials 13
13.1 - 13.24

14 PIONEER MUSEUM PLAZA
14.1 - 14.16
LYONS OFFICE
14.17 - 14.32

furniture 15
15.1 - 15.24

16 CONVERSATIONS
16.1 - 16.20

which the completed works of architecture are the publications, their seminal nature attested to by reviews and exhibitions. Candidates thus reflect on a body of work that is complete, while the consequences for future practice are explored in design work during the course of the PhD. This type of PhD was ideal for Bertram, who had been practising for ten years (including two years in Japan), had completed a Master's in 1997, and had finished a series of buildings with NMBW including the Somers House (2003), the Pioneer Museum Plaza Dimboola (2007), and the Elwood House (2008). As he explains, *I'd done a lot of projects and the task was really not to do more, but to try to tie them together.*

As a full-time staff member in the Architecture Program at RMIT since 2001, Bertram had collaborated with Shane Murray to develop the Urban Architectural Laboratory, initiated by Leon van Schaik; had published two books – *By-Product-Tokyo* (2003) and *Division and Multiplication: Building and Inhabitation in Inner Melbourne* (2002) – and had co-ordinated numerous design studios. This context of practice, research and teaching formed the ideal adjunct for design practice research, so while the duration of candidature is shorter than a standard PhD, Bertram felt as though he had been enrolled in the PhD for longer because of these structured activities.

We were, in our own minds, reasonably established in terms of what we were doing, so it was a good time to start because there was something to talk about – eight years of work. Because our practice is mixed with teaching, we're not churning out lots of projects like a commercial office and only take on projects we think are going to be useful. We have a particular attitude to each project, and a set of concerns that develop.

The PhD process began through a series of talks given as part of the design lecture series at RMIT. Although Bertram had developed a series of themes and questions for the PhD, he found it more difficult to work out a structure and an approach. He compiled a spreadsheet or matrix of all the possible things that he thought the work was predominantly about.

The A3 Excel spreadsheet became a useful tool. It was very boring, but it was an analytical device to work out this field of interrelated things. It helped me to be more specific about pulling out the differences between things, and what the really important things were, versus the not-so-important things.

Additionally for Bertram, a gifted and generous educator, the role of postgraduate study was explicitly perceived as a contribution to the architectural discourse rather than, as he says, *some sort of self-therapy or pure introspection. With this in mind, he reduced the possible number of themes to things he saw as generally applicable or generally useful.* For example, through the categories of detail, materiality and planning he was able to offer observations about *the act of construction, or how we think about the use of materiality, or about the decisions made by planning.* These issues existed not only in each of his projects, but also *in every architectural project – so that would then all be relevant to other people, not just to myself.*

Bertram explored his projects *in their own right, on their own terms.* That is, by removing them one degree from the myriad of factors beyond his control – other people involved, the site and the client – and making connections to other projects, he was able to:

reflect on what architecture is and what architects need to do…I was connecting into a general discourse on architecture and making it not just about our work or my work. I was trying to find ways in which to depersonalise it from the project and make it not just about that site or that person or that time but rather to be slightly more analytical.

Particularity and subjectivity were criteria that Bertram used for the selection and editing of themes. For example, *planning and the plan of a building* constituted two of Bertram's interests and were therefore selected above others. His emphasis here was on social relationships combined with abstract hierarchies of spaces.

They're two very particular and idiosyncratic things…so it doesn't include a discussion of geometry per se. On the other hand, every plan that an architect makes includes social structures and hierarchies between spaces. It's not comprehensive, but it is generally applicable. And then I would say, "Well, this is our particular attitude or intention within this."

The categories that Bertram privileged are topics that all architects have to deal with, regardless: *They can choose to suppress them or raise them, but still they're there.* So Bertram's and, indeed, NMBW's architectural expression, detail and materiality arise through very particular choices.

In a literal sense, each project has its own origins. The Somers House was looking at sheds because there were sheds on the site and we had never done a project that looked like a shed before. In Elwood, we looked at the fence because the fence was there and it was next to another fence.

The origin, therefore, is not necessarily as important as what is explored and done within that type of thing.

What became interesting was trying to work out, "Well, why this shed and not that shed and not that shed?" and, "Why this particular way of connecting things and not that?" Absolutely there's an editing process. "Why did we take a photo of this?" There's some sort of shared intuitive feeling that, "Yeah, that one's really great, but that other one's not!"

The research revealed these strategic collections and examinations across the spectrum of Bertram's work. For example, in the writing of *Division and Multiplication* co-authored with Kim Halik, Bertram notes:

There were a whole lot of things in the world that we were looking at, but in the end we chose 15 things because they were particularly pertinent in some way. There was a selection and a precise sorting into different groups that have some common threads and some differences within them.

Bertram's PhD research process was much the same:

There's all this stuff and I'm choosing ten things and then it's a matter of ordering and grouping those ten things to make an argument, just like Division and Multiplication was one argument out of this stuff that exists…it isn't exclusive. It's not like that material only exists in one form.

Thus the act of researching for the PhD became a familiar process of treating the work as found objects.

I found certain ways of showing them one way and not another way, without an idea of being complete or holistic. And so the ordering of a series of complex but interrelated pre-existing things into some new structure or order was really the task. It seemed very similar to the process of analysing, then representing a found condition in the world, which is what we do all the time.

A key moment occurred for Bertram during one of his Research Symposium presentations, roughly halfway through the PhD. He recalls: *It got serious because the panel was very good – there was Li Shiqiao, Richard Blythe and David Porter. They picked up on certain points that related and helped me pull together what were fairly different parallel inquiries at that point.*

One particular observation concerned Bertram's use of the term *precision*. What exactly was meant by the term? What was Bertram being precise about and why? This led to an important clarification, as he says; rather than precision being for its own sake or meaning *neat*, it concerned *looking at the points [in the world] where precision breaks down, where a certain sense of order fails to accommodate the situation and has to be adjusted. In Division and multiplication (2002),* the study investigated everyday inner suburban buildings as a response to anomalies between city planning rules and the rules of the buildings themselves. The collection showed a series of *on-the-edge-of-typical* buildings that revealed the typical by showing where it didn't work. The intent was to demonstrate a principle by looking at where it failed or had to be adjusted. Another example, the fence of the Elwood House, was similarly about being very accurate and faithful to the way a fence is made, but then at certain moments deviating from that to accommodate *new or non-typical conditions* of what was a very particular and idiosyncratic site.

I realised that unless you attacked the research with a certain degree of precision, you would never get to that point where you understood where it deviated from the normally precise case. You remain slightly blind to exactly how it was or wasn't typical unless you could describe and analyse that situation and draw it very precisely…It was a type of ironic precision – being precise in order to find the bits where it was loose. That made me think really hard about something I'd felt intuitively, that it was important to be very clear and definite about how something is made in relation to the way other things are made… There are some things which are continuous and others which get adjusted. It's working on a very micro scale in order to have an atmospheric effect or a change in mood or behaviour that is very fuzzy, as opposed to architecture that is very measured.

Bertram found the Research Symposium presentations a beneficial part of the process:

You present in front of very intelligent people who are there to try and analyse and find their own reading of what you're saying. Suddenly they'll say something that you had never thought of before and even if you don't use that exact thing, it prompts you to think about other things. It's like an injection of a new thought, and that doesn't happen very often.

While the impact of the PhD is yet to be completely revealed, given Bertram's recent completion, he has already found that the projects completed within the candidature have benefited from the clarity and focus demanded by the process.

DESIGN DOMAINS: THEIR RELATIONS AND TRANSFORMATIONS AS REVEALED THOUGH THE PRACTICE OF PAUL MINIFIE
COMPLETED: 2010

Paul Minifie has eighteen years' experience as a design architect on some of Australia's most significant public buildings and developments, which have attracted institute and other professional awards. Since founding his practice in 1999, significant work authored includes the design of the Centre for Ideas at the VCA and the Australian Wildlife Health Centre at Healesville Sanctuary, both award-winning projects that have forged the practice's innovative reputation. He is Associate Professor of Architecture at RMIT.

Paul Minifie, Associate Professor of Architecture and founding director of Minifie van Schaik Architects, was invited to engage in the Invitational design practice research program in 2008. Minifie and Nigel Bertram are the first practitioners to complete under these regulations, which Leon van Schaik has used to reinforce the research focus on design practice. Like Bertram, Minifie had reached a significant point in a career that has spanned across teaching, research and architectural practice. Several important buildings had been completed, including the Centre for Ideas, the Victorian College of the Arts (2003) and the Australian Wildlife Health Centre at Healesville Sanctuary (2004–2006). A series of unbuilt experimental projects had been published, such as Streaming Houses (2002); The Nine-Square Inflation project; the Manifolds project, incorporating Harbour and Corner Studies, and the Seven Pillars Taut Hypostyle project. Minifie, who has worked with ARM and Howard Raggatt during and just after his undergraduate studies, is a highly inventive and rather *heteroclitic* (deviating from ordinary forms or rules, irregular) architect. The work included in the PhD has a diverse set of themes and strategies, *some completely independent, some related either chronologically or expanding on other themes, many un-building-like, quite esoteric and experimental, never intended to become constructive pieces of work architecturally.* And the opportunity to reflect on his work to date was welcomed:

> *[I wanted] to see how the whole thing looks in the rear-view mirror and wondered how it changes what one might see looking forward...an important impulse was for it to be something of an engine that could carry one forward in an active and generative way, rather than merely tying up the loose ends and re-framing for public or dissertation purposes.*

Minifie's work and interests are unusual in that he is highly skilled with digital technologies, including the various scripting and animation softwares,

and is a self-confessed *amateur mathematician* – or at least someone who reads pure mathematical journals. Combined with this, his broad-reaching cultural and architectural knowledge allows him to view architectural discourse, including the emergent digital architectural inquiries, from a certain critical perspective. For example, while he sees many practitioners investing in the *emergent digital inquires* as if they provide a legitimating narrative for architectural outcomes, he borrows these techniques or processes from disciplines outside of architecture in order to shed light on architectural relationships such as legibility and process.

His undergraduate architectural degree was undertaken in the 1980s when post modernism and semantic systems dominated the discourse and as a result, he says, *I've never really been able to think outside of it. I can't think of things not functioning symbolically at some level in order for them to be comprehensible.* The concerns he therefore brought to the PhD, working explicitly from the position that architecture is more than its own internal discourse, were to bring *relationships of the physical attributes and properties of the building design that has some tangible or at least theoretical relationship back to a set of intentions which then has the ability to be legible or read in some way within the object.* He questions:

> *How, then, do those design actions end up being registered or impressed within the building, given that you could reasonably expect someone looking at the building to know certain things about why it was the way that it was – to infer, if not the deep intentions, at least something of the specifics of the generative act of bringing the building into being? That is an important part of my practice and it may sound as if all of architecture inevitably has to have those things, but I'm not sure that it does.*

The next part of this concern – or, as he says, *the set of relations* – is that if the first set of ambitions is achievable, *can the building talk beyond itself or beyond those relationships between the making of it and the theme? Can it talk to certain other things that exist within the world about the world and our functioning within it...?* The symbolic function of architecture is important to Minifie, firstly because it has the potential to open up connections between buildings and the world, and secondly because he sees many architectural discourses seeking to legitimate authenticity through something else. Of symbolism, he says,

> *So many architectural discourses are basically lying to themselves. They try never to use that kind of idea or term, but implicitly they always do. People who are totally into materialist discourse – "Just let the concrete be concrete and the wood be wood and zinc be zinc" – inhabit a purely symbolic realm of the concrete representing an idea, a representation of an idea. It's not a purely materialist thing and can never be anything other than symbolic. I think that discourse of authenticity relies on always being able to suppress the symbolic realm that you're working within. The digital emergence discourse, which my stuff fits into...and*

I'm not trying to disown, has certain qualities in it that try and pretend that things are happening at the level of pure phenomenon, but they're not really.

Through the PhD, Minifie hoped to identify certain things in his practice about which particular statements could be made that could not be made about other kinds of practice. As he says, *there's quite a lot of terminology invented to try and get at those ideas. Often things make more sense in distinction to other kinds of practices.* One such practice is mathematics.

My eye wanders across certain pieces of mathematical literature and scavenges things which seem like they might throw light on an architectural relationship – usually one that has become hackneyed and boring! But there does seem to be a rich parallel between the kind of things we'd like to describe about buildings and certain ideas described by mathematicians.

Injection is an idea taken from set theory that describes a relationship between two sets of objects where there is a singular relationship between one entity in one set and an entity in another set. Minifie sees this suggestion of mapping as potentially useful for architecture. *I was using that to say, well, if there's a specific enough quality to a building, then maybe there is some possibility that it can have an injection onto some other thing.*

Architectural composition – the conscious arrangement of things – was another topic that highlighted ideas of specific relationships and sets. Minifie's take is that, as an idea, composition is thought of and used in mostly conservative ways; *that is, architecture is a finite and bound language and novelty isn't really possible. What is possible is a continual re-organisation of these things, nuanced and different, but only when compared with the way that other people have arranged things before.* Minifie is convinced that this does not have to be the case, *You can still have the idea of composition without the notion that all the moves have already been pre-determined by this body of stuff, which has been canonically established as Architecture.*

Rather than thinking about the compositional elements themselves, for example *a whole set of little things about windows, column grids and things being on-grid or off-grid, sheer flat walls and then walls and points of columns being independent of each other and so on...* that signified high modernism, Minifie is interested in the relationship between these sets of things that follow a logic and have a spatial logic.

It's possible to make up new rules that can happen compositionally – what I call a Design Domain, which is a set of rules consistent with one another, making sense with one another, that let you design…You can still do an infinite number of different things - composition can still come to bear - it's just that there can be new kinds of spaces, new building instances.

Minifie's next line of thought was to determine what those things could be.

One way of making that in a very clear way is to have very clear reduced sets of relationships that make sense together - and so that's kind of the first bit of the design. Then there's this dilemma of how to actually make it into something which is legible and readable and I would call that 'composition' in the same way that one might in another kind of architectural discourse - it's just that you're working with new kinds of possible relationships between things. Trying to detail how that worked across a few different projects and buildings was an important part of the PhD. And then the more difficult thing was to try and work out why that particular stable configuration seemed more appealing than any of the other ones that could have been. I think I was only kind of partly successful in describing that.

Implicit in these arguments is Minifie's belief that relationships between things can exist independent of the sphere of their application: *so often people figure out clever things in order to solve a problem, but the way that they solve the problem then has a life of its own that can structure other things with many different fields of utility and purpose.* While Minifie roams far and wide in his practice, he insists,

I'm never really outside of the sphere of architecture… the interest is primarily architectural. It's just that interest can be sharpened, and certain of our dearly-held internal architectural beliefs can be re-focused by comparing and borrowing other sets of relationships as a way of testing what we tacitly believe about architecture.

Minifie stresses that the culture of the Research Symposia, of debate and of the communal nature of postgraduate research at RMIT was valuable.

Much of what I discussed in the PhD, both implicitly and explicitly, had been brought to my attention by the practices of my immediate peers or mentors or seniors within this particular community. So a lot of the PhD [reflected] implicit arguments I was having with other people; and the reason those arguments were important and [ones] that I could engage with was because I knew these people and I respected their work really deeply, and it's because of this that the discussion becomes meaningful for you within the body of the work in your PhD. Now I can imagine that most people in the world aren't doing that. Not architectural PhDs. They're having a conversation with the broad body of literature as it is sort of being 'sifted' and comes to them through studying via the web, and it just seems – compared with what we were doing – such a bloodless activity.

Nigel Bertram is one such peer with whom Minifie not only commenced and finished his Master's in 2002 but also his PhD. *It was a very beautiful experience, going through doing the PhD at the same time as Nigel. It would have been much more difficult without kind of being roped together in some strange way. And this was not because of the direct content of the work per se:*

There are enormous similarities in our attitude to architecture and how we feel about it. I mean, Nigel is such a realist; he believes that real things exist in the world and I don't really believe that real things exist in the world. I'm kind of an idealist, but Nigel is always trying to work out exactly why the world is like it is. It's like this sort of magical Marxist belief in the realness of things, whereas I'm sort of always wondering why the hell it isn't any of the other million ways it could possibly be! It's kind of an interesting parallel investigation.

COMPLETION
SEMINARS

... Twice a year candidates are asked to present their work-in-progress to panels, and these presentations are organically related to everyone's research work plans. Typically the initial Research Symposium presentation scopes the propositions arising from the candidate's review of past work; the second Research Symposium provides through project and literature reviews a survey of the enchainments in which that work was conducted; a series of intermediate Research Symposia cover tranches of project work devised to address research gaps identified between proposition and review; and in a penultimate Research Symposium – prior to their completion seminar at a final Research Symposium – candidates present the outlines of their catalogues, research catalogue, or 'durable visual records' together with their design for their final presentation through exhibition, web, film or performance.

Candidates present to panels made up of supervisors and external critics, but sessions are open to all, and all attending are invited to enter into the proceedings. Candidates present their work for up to half an hour, and in the remaining half-hour chairs of panels construct around that work the best possible conversation: a conversation that aims to help the candidate further their work.

[This is an excerpt from p. 18]

CHARLES ANDERSON
A landscape architect who has a distinguished reputation as an artist, designer and conceptualiser of public space and who has received numerous awards for his work.

RICHARD BLACK
An architect, Associate Professor at RMIT University, whose research explores the role of site in the architectural design process. This has been tested on case study locations along the River Murray floodplain, examining the interaction of built environments and the ecological process of the river.

STEPHEN COLLIER
An architect for over 20 years having worked on projects in Spain, Hungary, the Netherlands, Belgium and Australia. With a strong interest in practice-based design research combined with various teaching roles he has been the recipient of awards both here and overseas including several professional awards for design excellence in major residential and commercial projects.

GRAHAM CRIST
An Associate Professor at RMIT and Director of the design practice Antarctica, whose research has examined his practice in order to uncover its driving collaborative motives and technical innovations. He demonstrated an early application of 'off-the-peg' structures in design, applied as generous containers to the unpredictable interactions between users and inhabitants.

THOMAS DANIELL
A practising architect and critic based in Kyoto, Japan, who was the recipient of the RMIT Vice Chancellor's Award for an Outstanding Thesis in 2010 for his PhD *Negotiating Context*.

MELANIE DODD
An architect, urban designer and academic whose design practice and research interests focus on the relationships between social infrastructures and constructed urban environments between the lived and the built.

THEODORE KRUEGER III
An Associate Professor of Architecture at the Rensselaer Polytechnic Institute whose research interests include human-environment interaction, cognition and perception.

ROSALEA MONACELLA
A landscape architect and academic whose research focuses on the specialisation of emergent urban fields and the exploration of the diagram as a material operation, which considers the transformation of formal structures that adapt to the changing measures and orders of an urban landscape.

NICHOLAS MURRAY
An architect and sound designer who has researched a positive role for acoustics in architecture, a field in which acoustics are usually applied to suppress unwanted sounds. The research has profound implications for the design of learning environments.

YAEL REISNER
An architecture educator based in London whose research is captured in the book *Architecture and Beauty* (John Wiley & Sons, Chichester, 2009).

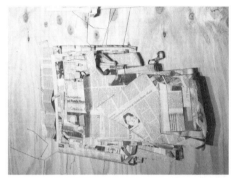

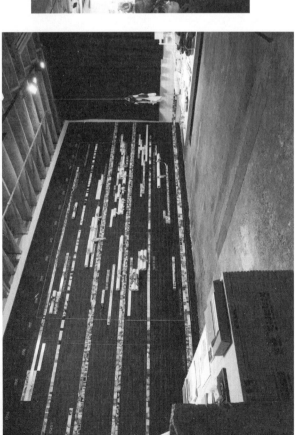

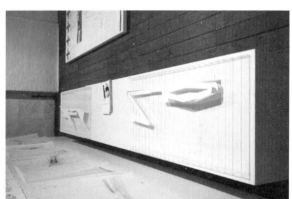

STEPHEN COLLIER

MELANIE DODD

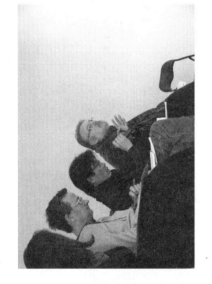

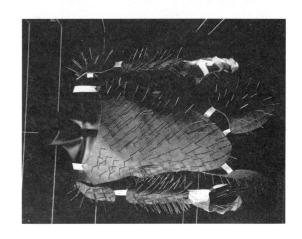

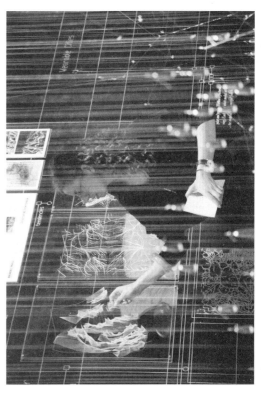

ON REFLECTION:
THE GRADUATE
RESEARCH
CONFERENCE

ANNA JOHNSON

The Critics: Reflections on Design Practice Research and the Research Symposium

At the most recent RMIT School of Architecture and Design Research Symposium, a discussion panel was convened called Reflections on Design Practice Research. This session, held after a full day of candidate reviews, brought together a number of the notable visiting critics, including Professors Marcelo Stamm, Johan Verbeke and Li Shiqiao, who, along with Professor Leon van Schaik and Head of School Richard Blythe, talked openly about the various stumbling blocks and poignant moments throughout the presentations that revealed the emergent and at times extraordinary originality of the work, but also the very essence of design research and of the Research Symposium events. As Li observed:

It's very interesting for a visitor, coming from far away, outside…this is not the normal thing that's happening around me. I find this really exciting, but at the same time I'm confronted with countless moments of provocation. Because (the issue) is really: how do you judge an act? We're really talking about not analysing design but judging the designing act as the real substance of the academic achievement. It comes to the point of stumbling blocks. We stumble – therefore we have to have the ability to recognise where and how and how many times we stumbled on the way, and this is really equally as important as high achievements… this kind of mastery-by-design was very much a medieval tradition in the sense that if you want to call yourself a master then you have to produce a masterpiece. I think this is an important step that we're innovating, but also restoring a form of humanity which is fundamental to human existence, which really is that we have created a condition within which we can make a judgement on what is a good designing act.

What began in late 1986 as a desire by the recently appointed Head of School Professor Leon van Schaik to have local architectural practitioners recognise the mastery of their work, and not regard it as somehow less than their international contemporaries by giving them the language to converse within the broader discipline and then to grow the professional knowledge base, has become a internationally renowned postgraduate design practice research program with over 100 candidates and dozens of visiting critics. In this postgraduate model, the research is not about design but rather is done in the medium of design itself.

Following his move to Australia, van Schaik searched for a model that would help facilitate his growing ideas. And it was after a conversation with a friend – a quantity surveyor who had been through a postgraduate program at the University in Birmingham, where it was explicit that the students didn't leave their place of work – that van Schaik conceived of the design practice research model. As van Schaik recalls, the program at Birmingham advocated:

> We want you to bring what you're doing at work into the critical framework of the program, and examine it in there, and then go back and keep doing it. And I thought, that's something that really should be happening in architecture... And so I had a series of meetings – I remember two meetings with about 30 architects each, at which I've put this as a proposition, and I added another thing to it; I said, "You owe it as a duty to your profession to actually grow the knowledge base of the profession as such, not the stuff that passes for research, which is very seldom of any particular interest to practitioners."

Van Schaik nutted out a structure and a set of presentation requirements and after the first cohort signed up – including Howard Raggatt, Michael Trudgeon, Allan Powell and Alex Selenitsch, among others – so began the rhythm of Research Symposium presentations and examinations. Van Schaik managed to attract some very high-profile and generous critics in this early stage, including Diana Agrest and Mario Gandelsonas. *Some of these [candidates] had never ever had this kind of conversation with the sort of people who were on the international circuit. Howard tried to talk over the top of Diana Agrest, who is tiny, and she just stood up and said, "Listen here, you – I am the critic, you listen to me! And proceeded to give him the benefit of her aggregated wisdom.* Beatrice Colomina and Michael Sorkin were also some of the early critics, with Sorkin being an examiner in that first round of completions. What was happening at these events, however, was *a mixture of people learning intensively from each other and listening to each other, and then getting this international critical discourse injected.*

Right from the start there was enormous encouragement from the visitors, who, as van Schaik recalls,

> were just amazed that practitioners with such accomplished work would actually subject themselves to this kind of process. They had never encountered anything like it anywhere else in the world. Predominantly at the beginning they were Americans and there still isn't anything like it in America. But they were also incredibly enthusiastic about it. They were in awe of the work, but they were enormously useful in heightening the ambition with which people examined their work, and extending their notions of what the intellectual frameworks might be. Two people who were really quite terrific early on particularly in that regard were Andrea Kahn and Kevin Alter, both academics from the United States.

The enrolments increased steadily each year, as did the audiences and Research Symposium events, which became increasingly sizeable and dynamic. Whereas the first group were largely practitioners, the next shift was towards practitioner academics and soon after this, in 2001, van Schaik realised the program needed to be expanded to include a PhD level as well. Drawing together a group including Nikos Papastergiadis, Paul Carter and Ranulph Glanville, van Schaik remembers that *between us we thrashed out a model, now known as the upside down cocktail glass. It's a conical diagram, with a straw going through it. And at the broad base of it there is an investigation of previous practice, which might very well be a Master's, and then there's the identification of the gap.*

This idea of the gap, an essential term for this research, came originally from Gerard de Zeeuw, then a professor from the University of Amsterdam who had been one of van Schaik's PhD examiners in 1987 and is another person whom van Schaik cites as being critical for the articulation of the PhD model:

> *His field of research was research! And he basically said the first act of a researcher is to draw a line. He gave a wonderful lecture - after somebody had shown about 200 slides, he stood up and he had one image, and it was a sheet of acetate on an overhead projector, and he said "The fundamental act of research is" - and he drew this line - "it's to draw a line and say, 'I'm looking at this, and not at that.'" And then he said, "And why am I looking at this? I'm looking at this because I believe there is a gap between what we understand about this now, and what we could understand about it."*

And so this term helped evolve the model as it is today, whereby candidates look at their past work and identify that gap. Typically this process is done three times within the PhD. As van Schaik explains:

> *They design themselves into a situation where they're either looking at what's going on in the office, or they're actually conducting theoretical projects, in order to fill the gap. Then they evaluate, redefine the gap, and have another go. And then at that point, you've learnt enough about filling the gap to be able to look back over the whole thing, and describe from the vantage of what is called 'the PhD moment', what it is that you've done. And it's called 'the PhD moment' because it is that point when you've reached that moment where you suddenly feel, "Yes, I can see all the way through it." You can then put a sampler down, and bring that out, and say look, that's what this has been about.*

Ranulph Glanville, theoretician of cybernetics and architecture, studied with van Schaik at the AA in 1969–71, later collaborating on various research and teaching projects. Working with van Schaik on a didactic model embracing full-scale fieldwork, digital approaches and bricolage assemblage, and formalising the difference between a design research Master's and a PhD, Glanville had a considerable role in the formation of the PhD design research stream. A regular critic and examiner at the Research Symposia, Glanville also second-supervised several of the first PhD candidates. For Glanville, the research-through-design model now established at RMIT,

> *begins from the notion of valuing design. If you look at a great deal of design research as it's done, it's done by people whose understanding of design is clearly not the understanding of a designer, and who very often wish to treat design as if it were something else. …So historians use architecture as material for historical analysis. They are using the subject not for what the subject is, but what they can get out of the subject of design.*

Glanville see that one of the problems for design and research is research and the academy becoming very specialised: *Science as a word used to mean knowledge…it has come to mean a particular kind of knowledge formed in a particular way, reflecting a particular worldview.*

This perspective, then, has come to dominate how research is understood:

> *A lot of what's happened in design, and particularly in architecture, has come about through being fraudulently quasi-scientific, or trying to be, which can really be traced at least to the 1956 Oxford conference on architectural education, whose agenda schools in the British-influenced world still follow – which is that notion that there are three parts to design: there's design science, there's design theory and things, and then there's the studio, which is the place where you synthesise all this knowledge. But that knowledge that designers have of design in itself is somehow lacking. There was a feeling that it was not scientific.*

Glanville sees that part of what van Schaik wanted to do and what he had done in his design practice research PhD program, was *to discover a designerly way of doing things, and to respect the subject and the approach of design, to accept the value of design as something which was different to science.* During this time, Glanville wrote a paper called *Researching Design and Design Research* (1999 MIT Paper) and one of the points he makes is that *there's no such thing as research which isn't designed. Research itself is design: you don't just set something up and do it, you modify it, you change it, you fiddle with it until it works, and then you look at the result and you learn from that and that changes things and you go back.*

His conclusion was that it is ridiculous to make design subject to the rules of research, when research is only possible because of design.

> *Designers are making the new. Designers change the world; they're not so interested in what is, so I distinguish knowledge of from knowledge for. What designers need is knowledge for changing the world, not knowledge of what it is. Scientists want knowledge of what it is. They want to tell us how things are. Designers want to change it. Design is not interested in describing what is, but changing what is. The second thing is, as you design something you learn something, all the time.*

Given that design is about making something new, it is design that comes first, and that's what Leon got onto: *that in practice, people are always making the new. They're getting on with it…as people say, "It's the solution that defines the problem.* As Glanville says, *the process for designers is post-rationalisation, whereas in science they pretend that the process is rationalisation and is logical… the scientists try to leave out the observer. Designers cannot leave out the observer. We're trying to make room for the observer, the designer, to get on and do his work.* For this model of research in creating the new, design comes first, and then understanding what that reveals about the nature of design and the subject comes second. And, as Glanville reflects, a lot of what they did in discussing and evolving this design research model was indeed like this.

> *A lot of what we did, which is of course a reflection on how the program was developed, is learning this by doing, by being involved so we are actually designing the understanding. So we go back to designing research, we design the understanding and that's how we also developed the program. It was a matter of design with everyone involved contributing and some of us co-ordinating it, and assembling it, and formalising it.*

Paul Carter was also an important contributor to the transition of the research to PhD mode. Van Schaik had already conceived of the Research Symposium as a way of creating mutual support structures between researchers who spent the rest of the year apart pursuing their practices. He then conceived with Carter of a way in which several PhD candidates could even more interactively support each other. This was critical at this phase in the program, as only van Schaik was qualified to be a senior supervisor of PhD candidates, and there was a university limit of seven candidates per supervisor. The group included Charles Anderson, Sand Helsel, Jenny Lowe, Gini Lee and SueAnne Ware. They shared an interest in unusual temporalities in practice, and van Schaik asked Carter to provide a critical text that could frame the conversations between these candidates. That text concerned ephemerality, and this group came to call themselves the *Ephemerals*. Carter co-supervised some of these candidates, and provided them with a robust intellectual framework during their research. This was a crucial moment in the development of the research program, but the need for it has fallen away as more of our staff have graduated and become supervisors in the Invitational stream.

Another key figure in the evolution of the PhD by design practice research model was Professor Nikos Papastergiadis, currently Professor in Cultural Studies at Melbourne University's School of Culture and Communication. Upon his return from working and living in England in 2000, Papastergiadis began working with van Schaik on various projects. As well as supervising his own students from 2001 onwards, Papastergiadis also became a regular critic.

> *Leon was very keen to incorporate not a purely theoretical perspective but a theoretical critique into the graduate program. He himself is someone who draws considerable energy from the interaction between theory and practice, between the history of ideas and the history of cultural and visual and architectural practices. This is one of the exciting aspects about the programs that he's developed – the way these traditions and trajectories are brought into a critical interface with each other. Obviously the base in this case is architectural practice, but there is a very rich sense of how ideas, whether they're explored and articulated in a visual or textual means, are often drawn from fundamental experiential issues or political engagements, and develop in critical relationship to different kinds of disciplines and practices. …So he and I share these core principles of believing that ideas come in multiple forms, but can stimulate each other by addressing the difference and the relationship between these forms whether they're text or the sketch or the moving image.*

For Papastergiadis, who sees a PhD really as an apprenticeship, reflects back on his own experience, and *the viva that I had for my PhD was one of the richest moments in my whole graduate life. It's a great luxury to have three or four people commenting on your work in a live context. And the more you're alive and open to the experience and the feedback, the more you appreciate it, rather than seeing it as a test.* For him *feedback* is a key word, rather than *assessment*:

> *The word 'feedback' in the language of complexity theory is a very dynamic process. It's the way in which you are enriched through the incorporation of external influences. It refers to the way in which everybody to some extent can critically select what they see and get from outside, and for me it would be fascinating to have another meeting with the whole panel in years to come, and see where it has gone, and to really test out*

whether this process has been a dynamic part of the evolution of the person's working practices and thinking model.

Papastergiadis works from the understanding that ideas come from interdisciplinarity. It is also *this intertextual procedure that is a critically important component.* Additionally, he sees the very idea of the feedback process and the fact that it is staggered throughout the duration of the candidature and not just at the end as being vital. And then, as he says,

running along these two points, between the intertextual and the feedback, is the necessity for both candidate and examiners to be sharing that early principle that examination and academic practice is not an exercise in policing, but an exercise in articulation. Making clear, making communicable, practices and insights and observations, and then testing and developing a language that other people can use, or refuse. In other words, it's open for contestation, open for application, open for examination by other people, so that the whole process is about how ideas are made real.

More recently, Papastergiadis has been involved in the development of the PhD by publication, another evolution of design practice research within the Invitational program, where the completed works of architecture are the publications and their seminal nature is affirmed by reviews and exhibitions. For him, what is interesting about this model is not to proceed towards a *celebratory kind of procedure whereby you say, "Oh look, this person has done X, Y and Z in the last ten or twenty years, and isn't it marvellous, and what a great achievement"…but what's more interesting is to try to figure out what more is within that practice that is of continuous relevance, that has vibrancy, that articulates some core set of ideas and beliefs.*

Papastergiadis has seen this being done quite well, but also sometimes rather awkwardly. However, this awkwardness is most interesting and revealing about the design practice research model because, in the end, candidates are brought closer to their practice. As he says:

Here the candidates have not quite articulated what it is that persists in their own practice. But they are aware that something is in there that they are continuously trying to get out, and it comes out in each new project, but it's not yet out fully. And in some instances they don't want to fully make that visible, for fear that once it's made visible it will somehow end, or the mystique will evaporate once it's put on the table.

However, as Papastergiadis asserts, the more the ideas and the work are articulated the more the research and thus the practice are strengthened.

The model is of value insofar as it makes visible something that's ongoing and deep and persistent in the mindset of the practitioner, rather than celebrating and monumentalising the past achievements. It's about trying to find out what the pulse is in a creative mind, and then strengthen that or deepen or extend it or enrich it in some way, rather than freezing it and putting a frame around it and giving it a big round of applause.

And so as one of the closing comments in the Reflections on Design Practice Research panel discussion, Professor Marcelo Stamm reflected:

I see these Research Symposia actually as very rare forum… Believe me, I've been to forty, fifty, sixty international conferences and I must admit I've hardly ever encountered a place where I saw so much genuine, direct… authenticity. I know this concept has currency and people think that there is no authenticity in the world, but I think there is if there is an honesty and a directness, if there is exposure of what you're doing: "Look, this is what I've got." Actually, the first thing I would always say when I sit on these panels is, "Thank you so much for agonising in the last three, four, five weeks about how will I present this and what will I say." There's so much work that goes into this. What this does, though, is this: the Research Symposium is a stage, is a space where you play a role that is not you. It allows you to get closer to who you may be…but it's a stage in the most noble Delphic sense…Know Thyself.

Plenary Comments

Research Symposia end with a Plenary Session at which improvements and commendations are gathered from the attendees: candidates, panel members and examiners. Through these sessions, the Research Symposium has been refined into the form that it takes today.

There were false starts. In 1988, the first format involved three Research Symposia per year. This soon proved incompatible with the working rhythms of practitioners – and when numbers increased, it was also incompatible with the academic calendar. In 1989 we moved to two Research Symposia per annum, in the study-break at the end of each semester.

At the outset too, timing was rather flexible: panels ran for as long as they sustained a conversation. Soon we were running parallel streams and the current lockstep timetable came into play to enable exchanges of panel members and the movement of observers from one stream to another, as their interest required.

Here as an example is a summary of the recommendations from the Research Symposium's Plenary Session of May 2004:

SUGGESTIONS FOR IMPROVEMENTS FROM CANDIDATES
AND STAFF INCLUDED:

→ Ensure that alumni of the Research Symposium and Adjunct Professors are invited to the weekends at the same time that candidates are invited.
→ Better Coffee.
→ Bios of all panel members, not just the ones giving public lectures.
→ Ensure that panels have a mixed disciplinary make-up (c/f previous demands for disciplinary coherence, esp. w.r.t. Landscape Architecture).
→ Is a panel of six too big? Chairs to consider having a primary panel whose views must be heard and a secondary one for further comment.
→ A timetabled time for people to meet to workshop, caucus and debate with their peers.
→ Maintain the Friday night banquet, but include more structured mixing events, perhaps a balcony party on the Saturday evening?
→ Reconsider the timing of the event to allow fuller undergraduate participation, while maintaining time-slots for visitors from USA and Europe.
→ Plea that Chairs keep to time. This is vital, as many panellists have to move between sessions, and many people need to observe work in different streams.
→ Plea that the Chairs of each panel makes clear statements about the position of candidates — that they are commencing, midway, or concluding.

→ Find ways of seeing what other people are doing — consider asking candidates to exhibit a poster of their work for the duration of the weekend.
→ Promote the event for thesis students.
→ Remind people that the research culture depends on their attending the conference, and fails them if they attend only their own session.
→ Inter-university links should be encouraged.

EXTERNAL VISITOR COMMENTS:

→ Continuing atmosphere of generosity and toughness praised.
→ Beware falling between research-by-project and research-by-thesis. In 'by project' research, the design begins at the outset, not after a thesis has been written…
→ Digital technology should no longer be taken as a category as such. Candidates should be in the steams appropriate to their projects, not the underlying technology.
→ Maturity of students is a boon, unique. VIP to maintain rigour in selection of candidates, because the general standard of engagement is far superior to that in other places where anyone who pays gets a place.
→ Ensure that all work references the body of knowledge built up by former candidates' work — most of which has been published by the School.

Most of these recommendations have since been implemented or have been used to refresh existing practice. Amongst these visitors, and making the final point above, was Professor Martin Woolley (then Research Dean at Goldsmiths College, now Director of Research, Central Saint Martins College of Art and Design) who also commended the Research Symposium process as being unique, central to the development of a research culture, and needing to be replicated across the world in design research. Over the years, other visitors have sought to capture their view that the Research Symposium is something new and important in design research:

At the October 2004 Plenary Session, Professor John Frazer (then Head of School, Hong Kong Polytechnic University, now Queensland University of Technology) said that the Research Symposium continues to be a model for other educational institutions, like the Royal College of Arts and the Bartlett, who continue to get it wrong. The model should be further promulgated, though there is resistance to hearing about it in the north.

Professor John MacArthur (University of Queensland, now Head of School and Dean at same) pronounced the Research Symposium a very rewarding experience.

In May 2005, Craig Bremner (then Head of School of Architecture, University of Canberra, now Charles Sturt University) commented on the differences in the ten years since he last participated. The shift from Master's to PhDs, a richer mix of streams, a more organised event, and yet the nature of the undertaking and its breadth remains the same. The openness of spirit is intact, has not closed down. Still a vital and dynamic part of Australian culture.

Professor Jonathan Hill (then a Reader at the Bartlett School of Architecture UCL, now Professor of Architecture and Visual Theory at same) commented that he had enjoyed the energy and innovation he had experienced – feeling it very analogous to the Bartlett. He argued that there were tiny things that could improve, but that the Research Symposium really works very well indeed. Research questions must be stated clearly, even when starting with a body of work. Writing as a creative tool in its own right could play a greater role. Nonetheless the standards of writing and drawing of the candidates was at a very high standard. It was fascinating to see different histories and landscapes playing through the work. The generosity and openness of the Research Symposia is great, but it is very strange that neither supervisors nor candidates are apprised of the recommended results at the end of an exam; this is routine at UCL. He strongly recommended that a way be found to do this here. (Since implemented at RMIT.)

Alvise Simondetti (Arup, now leading their Virtual Design Network) described how valuable an event like this was to him in his search for future colleagues. He applauded the approach of conducting projects within such an academic framework. He suggested that it was time that the Research Symposium – such a terrific synchronous event – had an asynchronous afterlife through the web. (Implemented in part.)

At the Plenary Session of June 2006, no suggestions for improvements were made! There was a consensus that current settings should be maintained. Comments included satisfaction with: timing of sessions, length of candidate presentations at 20 minutes, feedback time proportions, absence of *in camera* deliberations, examination venue (except that it is not collocated with work in progress reviews) and the format of the weekend, including exams prior to weekend, drinks and lectures on Friday night, informal talk and drinks on Saturday evening and the Plenary Session on Sunday evening. Comments from guests included:

Professor Johan Verbeke (then Head of School of Architecture at Sint-Lucas, Belgium, now Director of Research at same): *Most impressed and a very high quality of exams. People coming together from so many disciplines and fields of work, practitioners and academics. Networking very evident. At the Master's level the close connection to practice is very impressive. Had heard about all of this, but seeing is believing. PhD research is impressive because projects are used to give authority to research. A positive atmosphere and climate evident all the way through, and impressive conversations between people in intervals, etc. Clearly all of this triggered by the people at RMIT.*

Professor Zeynep Mennen (Middle East University of Technology, Ankara): *Surprised by the strength of the research culture. Evident here is a different role for the university,* designed to be a fulcrum between the city and the academy, between practice and research. This is creating a different knowledge. Almost everywhere else there is an unbridgeable mutual contempt between practitioners and academics. Here the design research rift is bridged. In most technical universities, dominated by engineering culture, architecture is the black sheep. Here design research has succeeded inside the institution and outside. The sense of a community of practice and academy at the Research Symposium is palpable. Here the university gathers in energy and disperses it - never seen anything like this before anywhere - USA, Europe, etc. First-class work. Met wonderful people, will keep in touch.

Professor Kate Heron (Head of School of Architecture, University of Westminster): *Applauds what Zeynep has said and agrees. Recognises exactly the mutual support between candidates who could be competitors. Experienced two streams and found them very interesting. Found Research Symposium inspiring and energising.*

In October 2006, Terry Rosenberg (Senior Lecturer in Design, Goldsmiths College, London): *Observing three streams, each with its own inflections, I can say that you lead the field in practice-based research. I have taken away more than I have contributed, have benefited from seeing the contextual building and framing of work. You must capture and export this, blow your trumpet, let us know what you are doing, let people know.*

Dennis Sheldon (Gehry Technologies): *This is my first visit to the Research Symposium - I hope to come nine more times! Because there is nothing like it anywhere else in the world. Postgraduate research, especially at PhD level, is lonely everywhere else - seven years in a closet. The pedagogical thinking is hardwired into the Research Symposium; the idea that the students describe where they are in the program, where they are in their research schedule is very important. The Research Symposium and the components it brings together (SIAL, etc.) make RMIT the epicentre of innovation in the world today, a stellar program in the world, at Media-Lab level - you must market it! Consider what you are on the world stage; think how you can communicate this. It has been a great three days, and it came as a surprise to me, and it should not.*

Professor Ayse Senturer (Professor of Architecture, University of Technology Istanbul): *The Research Symposium carries people to a creative position, an intimate research. It is empathetic to candidates providing understanding of their ways of thinking, not just to their finding their own languages as designers. The synergies are very good. As is normal at commencement, it is difficult initially to find the main idea, the main concept, but this is normal. There is a big amount of knowledge inside each of us; the Research Symposium process of self-discovery, basing research on personal histories in practice, is a very good approach to recover the knowledge laid down by experience.*

At the May 2007 conference, Nicholas Ray (Director of Studies and Emeritus Reader, Department of Architecture, Jesus College, University of Cambridge): *A privilege to attend; I have learnt more than I have contributed. The Research Symposium addresses as nowhere else that I am aware of the 'Enlightenment problem' – that split between art and science – and it does this by embedding its research in practice. These PhDs are a learned and rigorous record of a journey in which the scientific and the artistic are shown transforming practice. The levels of criticism ensure that this is not merely a cataloguing nor an indulgent account of personal creativity.*
    Professor Teal Triggs (Head of Research, London College of Communication, University of the Arts, London): *A very pleasurable experience; will have to come back. So many presentations are cross-disciplinary; it would be good if the audiences moved between streams.*

In October 2007, following the conference, Professor Tom Barker (then Royal College of Art, now University of Technology Sydney): *The Research Symposium is intellectually stimulating, enjoyable and has an unusual cross-over between disciplines, certainly one that [I am] not used to in London. The diversity of design research at PhD level is very impressive...the Research Symposium is a well-orchestrated way of fostering research – would like to engage the RCA in collaborations with RMIT – in specific research projects and in two-way associations with the Research Symposia. Delighted, impressed: carry on.*
    Professor Kate Heron (Head of School of Architecture, University of Westminster): *Terrific process. Noted on last visit the generosity of engagement between practitioners – who might well be in direct competition outside – within the Research Symposium. Hope that a way can be found to extend the process internationally so that it can be used more widely. Would like to see links to governmental programs like CABE peer review in the UK, to systematic peer review processes in big offices...*

In October 2008, Professor Jeremy Till (Dean, School of Architecture and the Built Environment, University of Westminster): *I'll pitch in...this is the first time I've been, I've heard about it across the ponds, and I do think it's an amazing circumstance. It's both generous – the way people dispose themselves – and unique, as I know and*

I think that in many ways it shows the vitality of the research culture here, and to bring that to the surface in such a manifest manner is brilliant, I think. (He went on to warn about becoming a hermetic self-referential culture.)

Professor David Porter (then Head of School, Macintosh School of Architecture): *This has been a kind of scouting mission, for two reasons. One is I work in Scotland, which has a small and interesting architectural culture that is growing and when I became aware of what was happening here, the making an architectural and design culture, I thought that given where I'm coming from this is quite appropriate. Jeremy congratulated you on the building of your research culture and I would say yes, and I would also congratulate you on the contribution that this action is making to Melbourne and to Australia in terms of the development of architecture and design culture and I think it's very significant in that respect... I think that something Jeremy said, which is that in the extraordinary generosity of what is here, there could become a comfortableness – I don't think there is one, but there could be. There needs to be vigilance against that.*

In May 2009, Dr Felicity Scott (Assistant Professor of Architecture, University of Columbia): *I've been to Australia many times, but this is the first time I've been here for the Research Symposium, and I'm very thankful to Leon for inviting me and giving me an opportunity to be a part of this quite remarkable institutional project of re-thinking the PhD, or producing a platform for this type of critical reflection through practice.*

Professor Li Shiqiao (then Associate Professor of Architecture, Chinese University Hong Kong, now Weedon Professor in Asian Architecture, University of Virginia): *There are people out there who are intensely interested in this, and as something that a lot of people always wanted to speculate they could do, but there were too many institutional or collegial or cultural pressures to prevent them from doing something like this.*

William L. Fox (Director, Centre for Art and Environment, Nevada Museum of Art): *I've actually been looking for a university, since the first time I came here, in which to plant the seed of this idea for the arts community of North America, and Arizona State University, which is a large research university that is almost the size of RMIT, is now seriously looking at this. So Leon, all of you, it's an idea you've put forth that, once again, North America needs to be learning from Australia – it's a perfect example.*

Professor Tom Barker (then Royal College of Art, now University of Technology Sydney): *I would say now, I mean I've felt for the last couple of years, I've travelled around the world a lot, the* culture and community that you've built – Leon, Richard and everybody else – is the strongest design research community I've found anywhere on the planet.

In October 2009, Professor Andrew Brennan (Chair of Philosophy, La Trobe University): *I came back a second time and I started to understand what was going on here and I thought this is definitely right. I've got to make this happen at La Trobe. So now this is my third visit and it is now happening at La Trobe, I'm glad to say, because they put me in charge of graduate research there so I'm forcing it to happen. And so the good news is that something happening here, at RMIT, is now having this ripple effect throughout the rest of Melbourne to start with.*

Ashley Hall (Deputy Head, Department of Innovation Design, Royal College of Art): *I go to conferences a lot but a couple of days here is worth three weeks of conferences anywhere else. It's really tremendously stimulating, it's tremendously exciting and it's something I get enormous amounts from. I very much hope the candidates get a little bit from me. It's fantastic. It's much better than a conference and it's got to be maintained.*

In June 2010, Professor Jane Rendell (the Bartlett School of Architecture): *I just wanted to add a comment. This is my first visit and I very, very much enjoyed it and just the particular qualities that I noticed because I would agree with the last comment that practice-led research or design-led research isn't necessarily quite so new within the field of art and design and architecture [NB: at a symposium on design research at Westminster in 2009, Jonathan Hill and Murray Fraser acknowledged that this approach was initiated at RMIT in the 1980s] but I think there's something very particular about what's going on here that has a very special energy and one thing which I've really enjoyed. We also have a design PhD, but at the end of the process our design PhD still exists only within a bound document and I think the fact that isn't the case here and the exhibition component is so important gives a kind of freedom to the design and it kind of removes it from that academic model in some ways. I've really learnt a lot and also think this particular event is really special because again at the Bartlett, the PhD exam is a private event with two examiners, maybe the supervisor and the student, and it doesn't build a community in the way that you have here and I think the experience I've had over the last couple of days of just being on the panels with different kinds of experts constantly moving in different constellations of knowledge has just been fantastic and I think the interdisciplinary nature of the conversations is absolutely wonderful – having philosophers, having artists, having landscape designers, as well as architects. So I've really enjoyed it and I do think the Research Symposium is a really key aspect to building the program, building the community and especially the relationship with the profession – that seems so key that the professionals come into the academic environment and really want to learn from it and that dialogue between the professional and academia seems to me incredibly special.*

In October 2010, Professor Murray Fraser (then Westminster University, now the Bartlett School of Architecture): *It's been excellent; it's been really quite impressive. Leon has asked me several times before but I never could do it because of timing. So I came this time and I thought there were suspiciously good candidates to look at. It was like a dream. Having seen the quality of the work I've thought this model, this practice-based or practice-embedded, objects-based model is really, really impressive. It seems to be undoubtedly, from my experience from being here, the real distinctive quality, the real strength of the Doctorate program, certainly within architecture here. Both Nigel Bertram and Paul Minifie are fantastically good PhDs and a very, very impressive Master's from Robert Simeoni, which one could imagine could become an equally impressive PhD as well. In terms of publishing, I'm now starting a new design research series and I've been very happy to talk to PhD candidates to help them with publishing their research.*

Professor Claus Peder Pedersen (Dean of Research, Aarhus School of Architecture): *It's been a very inspiring and interesting experience. It has been really wonderful to experience the, in some cases, challenging array of practices that you are presenting here. One thing that wasn't too difficult to recognise was the quality here of people involved in the system. I'm really impressed by that and this openness towards letting the student's PhD work unfold a logic through investigating what was the essential thing, not falling back into simplified categories or an overarching academic framework. I found that part in this experience the great consideration of trying to draw that essence out of the projects that were presented. It's quite a challenge to how to do that. I think really we have a lot to learn from your way of doing that. So I would say our enthusiasm for going on with … this central ambition for working out how to incorporate the knowledge that is being produced outside of architectural schools inside the schools, that that should be part of our research body.*

2015

Dr Denise Sprynskyj researched the internationally acclaimed fashion practice S!X, known for its re-construction of tailored garments. She revealed the way that this practice uses an archaeological approach to its archive of garments, terms and places. She uncovered a new way of scripting design that captures ideas verbally and visually simultaneously.

Dr Peter Boyd researched the internationally acclaimed fashion practice S!X, known for its re-construction of tailored garments. He focussed on the design environment of the practice, revealing the uses of spaces real and imagined as generating incubators of design ideas and as a means of disseminating new and re-conceived garment collections.

Dr Fleur Watson studied the evolution of her practice as a curator of architecture and design. Comparing her innovations with those of her peers locally and internationally, she established new forms of performative agency that can advance the understandings and participations of audiences with the processes of making design ideas.

2016

Dr Tim Greer investigates his projects for architectural thinking permeated by a Cultural Continuum. He concludes that architecture can be open-ended, resonating with history but anticipating an evolving, mysterious complex of societal values, to accommodate future usage.

Dr Peter Tonkin researched thirty years of his architectural practice. Four seminal projects highlight the unusual nature of the work and are shown to be a materialisation of ideas and forms specific to place, each making an eloquent whole that develops a relationship to the continuum of architectural thought.

Dr Jan van Schaik researched the ways in which his practice creates design propositions that capture program requirements and the imagination of commissioning clients, often complex groups. 'Breugelage' conveys how teeming intelligences are brought together to create outcomes that surprise and delight clients, create work opportunities and produce learning environments.

Dr Petra Pferdmenges' research explored the manner that public space may be activated through participatory, temporary acts of architecture. Through the establishment of a research focused design practice she developed strategies and techniques that progressed traditional boundaries of architecture to seek new ways to facilitate social empowerment of marginalised communities.

Dr Anthony Hoete examined his practice, WHAT architecture, and identified that this be considered a 'Game of Architecture' governed by rules and constraints. Re-played through the frame 'Game of Housing', the research outcome proposes then actions an operating fieldwork of rules and roles to enable and empower architects to be 'game-changers'.

Dr Sebastian Penfornis explored the notion of play in his practice of landscape architect. The research revealed new modes of engagements (gardens), and artefacts (collages, models, drawings). The findings contribute to provide insight on making visible a significant part of the tacit knowledge in the field of landscape architecture.

Dr Erieta Attali interrogated twenty years of practice in landscape and architecture photography by tracking the evolution of her visual language, revealing how her practice is informed by specific motifs, which expose the continuity between landscape and architecture. Simultaneously, the research reveals photography as a powerful tool for interpreting built space.

Dr Nicholas Boyarsky explored ludic practices in architecture and urban design. The research focussed on the work of his practice. The research was structured by the recto and verso devices of deltiology. The outcomes provide insight into contingent and bottom-up design processes, the detail, and the model of expanded practice.

Dr Peter Brew explored the function of Idea in Architecture. Exemplars are considered to reveal the attributes, mechanisms, incentives, techniques and ideas as they are used by architects. This is suggested as a disciplinary model for architecture that considers the formulation and use of ideas to be a current field for design research.

Dr Roger Kemp investigated a relational approach to interior design practice. The research produced a set of tools and techniques for negotiating the perceived and experienced physical and virtual conditions of interiors. The outcomes provide a methodological catalyst for an expanded engagement in the design of our contemporary urban environment.

Dr Anthony Fryatt investigated a mediated approach to interior experience. The research produced diagrammatic and scenic tools that allowed for a performative and subjective production of interior relations. This positions the interior as a critical social tool, implicated in the production and exchange of our individual and collective identities.

2017

Dr. John Brown investigated the development of Future Adaptive Building to create a flexible, high quality domestic environment for people as they grow old. The research developed three architectural strategies for enhancing independent age-in-place living. The results provide insight into new roles that architects can play in an aging world.

Dr Sam Kebbell examined the design processes, motivations, and context of his own architectural practice in Wellington. His research revealed the creative potential of a tension between rarefied international ideas and more common local traditions. The findings contribute to a broader understanding of creative practice in architecture.

Dr Simon Pendal developed a new understanding of architecture that is atmospheric. This model establishes how direct experience, deep-time affiliation and one's imagining of new spatial possibilities might vibrate in harmony. These findings enhance our understanding of making places that carry a charge and continue to linger once visited.

Dr Robert Simeoni (Melbourne) explored the way his process of observing and capturing moments of spatial intervention in his neighbourhood informs his design practice. Through collection and reflection, the images and writing within this document exhibit and highlight the importance and value of spending time to document and understand sources of architectural inspiration.

Dr Steve Larkin makes evident deep connections that exist between two modes of practice, traditional Irish music and architecture. These modes are often casually linked but have not heretofore had their inter-connectedness demonstrated at a practice level. They evidence a particular contextual practice that explores Irish cultural landscapes.

Dr Michael Banney researched his design methodology. He discovered three ways in which he creates and uses anecdotes in developing design strategies. Stories are retrieved from his archive of memories or spontaneously engendered in real time. Others speculate future possibilities. The interweaving of these in design is a new insight.

Dr Simon Twose explored how architecture can have the poetic possibility of a sketch; how built space, like drawings, can prompt open questions. Strategies of poetic open-ness were distilled from a body of work. The research demonstrated the power of sketchy indeterminacy in creating new knowledge through architectural practice.

Dr Toby Reed's research discusses architectural ways of world-making and reality-construction. This practice-based PhD argues for an anti-representational account of the conscious and sub-conscious aspects of experiencing and designing architectural space, using the notions of black hole, screen-vortex and space-junk as a novel heuristic to investigate a versatile Melbourne-based architectural practice.

Dr Andrew Clancy (Dublin and London) tracked in their design process the conversations with his partner and with makers. He identified the ways in which ideas generate other ideas, sometimes fading away as they draw and model, and in other cases returning. He identified parallels with lost armatures in sculpture. The research documents with new clarity the conversational structure of collaborations.

Dr Cameron Bruhn researched the trajectory of Australian architecture, landscape architecture and interior design through the mediums of writing, editing and publishing. The research provides evidence of his contribution to local and international knowledge in publishing and the built environment, and demonstrates the development of innovative, cross-platform editorial techniques and structures.

Dr Cian Deegan researched the contexts that support the work of his joint practice. He discovered that the local decorum of place and personal spatial history are charged by infusions of exotica. These fascinations arise from concatenations of site and program. Thus other material cultures add richness to the work.

Dr Peter Cody subjected his practice to forensic analyses, building a case for the practicality of useful fictions. He discovered that the mental spaces captured by fictions transcend linear logic and enable the engagement of the totality of a practitioner's architectural intelligence. This enables designs that are rich and grounded.

Dr Colm Moore researched the underlying dynamics of his joint practice. He identified an unprecedented manner of establishing figures at the cusps between the constraints of sites, programs and ideas. He demonstrated how these figures are found and choreographed in the design process and how tensions are transformed into architecture.

Dr Alice Casey (Dublin) researched the modes of design in her practice, revealing especially how details are developed in a conversation between design idea, what other architects have built and a contractor's capabilities. She describes how analysis has built a platform for future, more complex work; and for teaching design. These outcomes are replicable by others.

Dr Denis Byrne researched the frameworks that motivate his practice. His analysis revealed three lenses through which design decisions are evaluated. Designs progress when at all scales they support communal activity; release social potentials and construct significant, meaningful movement. Design moments of each kind are captured in unusually evocative images.

Dr Leanne Zilka explored the aesthetics, techniques, and construction of fashion and textiles to develop ways to design and fabricate architectural objects and space differently. The research, undertaken through original design projects, provides insights and techniques that traverses from the scale of material and garment to that of rooms and buildings.

2018

Dr Corbett Lyon examined the mental spaces that he occupies when designing. His research reveals a correspondence with the mental spaces that he enters when learning to perform new music. In both cases a repository of past experiences and exemplars sits alongside pragmatic, procedural spaces. Connections previously suspected are demonstrated.

Dr Siobhan Ní Éanaigh researched her practice McGarry Ní Éanaigh Architects, Dublin, Ireland. This practice has transformed the designing of schools, finding ways to suffuse them with spaciousness inflected by saturated colour. The PhD reveals how by working in multiple mediums the architect creates new relationships between space, hue and tone.

COPYRIGHT & PERMISSIONS

BIBLIOGRAPHY

Schaik, L van & London, G 2010, *Procuring innovative architecture*, Routledge, London.

Schaik, L van & Spooner, M (eds.) 2010, *The practice of practice 2: research in the medium of design*, RMIT Press, Melbourne.

Schaik, L van 2008, *Spatial intelligence*, Wiley, Chichester.

Schaik, L van 2006, *Design city Melbourne*, Wiley-Academy, Chichester.

Schaik, L van 2005, *Mastering architecture: becoming a creative innovator in practice*, Wiley-Academy, Chichester.

Schaik, L van (ed.) 2003, *The practice of practice: research in the medium of design*, RMIT Press, Melbourne.

Schaik, L van (ed.) 2000, *Interstitial modernism*, RMIT Press, Melbourne.

Schaik, L van (ed.) 2000, *Ruins of the future*, RMIT Press, Melbourne.

Schaik, L van (ed.) 1995, *Transfiguring the ordinary*, Printed Books, Melbourne, 1995.

Schaik, L van (ed.) 1993, *Fin de siècle? and the twenty-first century: architectures of Melbourne*, RMIT Press, Melbourne.

Barnacle, R & Usher, R 2003, 'Assessing the quality of research training: the case of part-time candidates in full-time professional work', *Higher Education Research & Development*, Vol. 22, No. 3, pp. 345-358.

Bertram, N, Murray, S & Neustupny, M 2003, *By-product Tokyo*, RMIT University Press, Melbourne.

Bertram, N & Halik, K 2002, *Division and multiplication: building and inhabitation in inner Melbourne*, RMIT University Press, Melbourne.

Carter, P 2004, *Material thinking: the theory of practice of creative research*, Melbourne University Press, Melbourne.

Downton, P 2003, *Design research*, RMIT University Press, Melbourne.

Papastergiadis, N 2006, *Spatial aesthetics: art, place and the everyday*, Rivers Oram Press, London.

ACKNOWLEDGEMENTS

COVER

Photo of completion seminar for Graham Crist, 2 June 2010, Guildford Lane Gallery, Melbourne. Examiners: Stephen Loo, Felicity Scott, Li Shiqiao; Chair: Vivian Mitsogianni.

LEON VAN SCHAIK AO

Emeritus Professor Leon van Schaik AO, B.Arch. Studies (Ncle), AADip (SADG), M.Arch (UCT), PhD (CNAA), RIBA, LFAIA, LFAA,School of Architecture and Urban Design, RMIT, has written books on spatial thinking, the poetics of architecture and the processes involved in procuring innovative architecture. The practice-based design research program that he initiated in 1987 has become a template for institutions worldwide. His support of local architectural cultures and his leadership in the procurement of exemplary architecture has resulted in some of Melbourne's most distinguished contemporary buildings. He is a founding member of the Academic Court of the London School of Architecture.

ANNA JOHNSON

Phd (RMIT) BArch Hons (RMIT), BAppS (UC) Anna Johnson is a senior lecturer in architecture with RMIT School of Architecture & Urban design. Her research, teaching and design practice has been concerned with Asian Urbanism, relationships of landscape, context and architecture, as well as in narrative and architecture. She is also an author with several books published on Architecture. Urban Sanctuary and Living in The Landscape co-authored with Richard Black published by Thames & Hudson 2018 and 2016 respectively, are her most recent.

IAN NAZARETH

Ian Nazareth is an Architect, Lecturer and Industry fellow at the School of Architecture and Urban Design, RMIT University. His current research and design practice focusses on emergence and emulation in urban and architectural form. Ian contributes extensively to architectural media and critical design discourse. He is also the director of traffic.